Drawing Directors
Randal Kleiser

Volume II

Drawing Directors: Volume II

Editor & Cover Design: Mani Perezcarro

© Randal Kleiser Productions, 2025

All rights reserved.
No part of this book may be reproduced or transmitted in any form or by any means, electronic or mechanical, including photocopying, recording or any information storage and retrieval system, without permission in writing from the author.

www.randalkleiser.com

ISBN: 979-8-9886005-3-4

This book is dedicated to my parents, John and Harriet Kleiser,
who sent me to USC Film School when I was 18.

Foreword

I will never forget the first time I met Randal Kleiser. It was in New York—or maybe Los Angeles, I can't remember. But suddenly, there was an electricity that filled the room. Everyone became quiet. The room went dark. All our watches stopped. Okay, maybe that didn't happen. But there is something very powerful about Randal, and it's not the kind of bravado you might expect from the director of some of Hollywood's most iconic and beloved films.

Randal has a calm, generous presence that immediately puts you at ease. He doesn't command attention by raising his voice—he draws people in by listening. Really listening. He sees things others miss. He observes life with a painter's eye, and then he tells stories that resonate—whether it's a timeless summer romance like *Grease*, the family-friendly adventure of *Flight of the Navigator*, or the groundbreaking virtual reality storytelling of *Defrost*.

I remember being a little nervous the first time I brought up *Top Secret!*—specifically our shameless parody of *The Blue Lagoon*. I thought I should start with an apology. But instead, Randal laughed and completely embraced it. That's who he is—open, curious, and never precious about his work.

Over the years, I've come to know Randal not just as a talented director but as someone who is constantly seeking new ways to tell meaningful stories across every form and format. He's never stopped innovating, never stopped learning, and—most importantly—never stopped listening. And that, I think, is where the real magic lies.

Jerry Zucker

In this second volume of drawings, I continue to pay tribute to fellow directors I admire. Sketching them from life in various settings has been a hobby that has lasted for almost six decades. I have had the good fortune to meet most of them, and some have become good friends. I know how hard it is to make a movie, and the men and women in these pages have all done it with talent and style.

Randal Kleiser

JJ Abrams

When JJ decided to enter the film industry, his father, Gerald, a prominent television producer, advised him not to study film but to learn what to make films about. Taking his father's advice, JJ focused on storytelling rather than initially developing a distinctive style, like those of his heroes, John Woo and Brian De Palma.

In his senior year, JJ wrote a script that became the feature film *Taking Care of Business*. This launched a wunderkind career that included writing and producing *Regarding Henry* and *Forever Young*, as well as contributing to the pre-production of *Shrek*. His passion for directing emerged early, even earning him a small on-screen role as "Video Photographer #2" in the remake of *Diabolique*. In the scene, his character directs a parent to look misty-eyed for a promotional school video.

I first became aware of JJ when I saw his film *Cloverfield*. What impressed me was the seamless blend of handheld home video with state-of-the-art visual effects. In a groundbreaking sequence, a low-resolution video camera shoots the Statue of Liberty's head bouncing down a New York street. This had never been done before and gave a reality to the images that would not have been the same with the regular high-end Hollywood treatment.

As I watched more of his work, I noticed he was developing his own style. Lens flares appeared in almost every shot, starting with his 2006 movie *Mission: Impossible 3*. He went on to include them in *Super 8* and *Star Trek Into Darkness*. (You can watch a compilation of all these shots on YouTube.) In an interview with Stephen Colbert, JJ revealed that his wife asked him to stop using them after watching a moving scene from *Star Trek* where she could hardly see the actress.

After Carrie Fisher passed away, JJ cleverly pieced together outtakes from *Star Wars: The Force Awakens* to write new scenes that allowed her character to continue in the saga and wrap it up in *Star Wars: The Rise of Skywalker*.

Following in his father's footsteps, JJ stands as one of the most prolific producer-directors in the industry today. His IMDb page is always filled with projects ready to launch. Additionally, he has personally composed the themes for most of his TV series.

When asked by students how to get started, he says, "Make your movie. With today's technology, there's no longer anything stopping you."

Ben Affleck

Childhood friends Ben Affleck and Matt Damon started their film careers as extras in *Field of Dreams*. Fast forward a few years, and the duo was watching the Academy Awards from the set of *Good Will Hunting*, the film they wrote and starred in. At that moment, they couldn't have imagined that just one year later, they'd be on that very stage, holding Oscars for Best Screenplay.

The story behind their rise reminds me of Sylvester Stallone insisting on starring in *Rocky*. Like Stallone, Ben and Matt turned down launching the project until they were guaranteed the control they wanted—and it paid off big. Not only did they win their Oscars, but the film also received eight other nominations. They took their mothers to the ceremony and were thrilled when Billy Crystal performed a song with lyrics referencing them.

In 2000, I visited Michael Bay on the set of *Pearl Harbor* in Hawaii and watched Ben shoot a scene. I didn't actually meet him until years later at a poolside celebration at the Beverly Hills Hotel for his Oscar-winning film *Argo*. I was struck by how tall he was. I expressed my admiration for his work on this masterful picture. As director, producer, and star of *Argo*, Ben was able to create an exciting, dramatic, and surprisingly funny movie based on an untold true story. The docudrama style combined the zaniness of Hollywood with a solid political thriller. At the party, I also ran into John Goodman, and I congratulated him on his performance as the jaded makeup artist. Ben also guided hilarious turns by Alan Arkin as the cynical producer and Richard Kind as the hapless writer of the nonexistent production.

To ensure authenticity for his film *Air*, Ben personally shot various formats such as Super 8, 16mm, and three-tube video cameras from the early '80s to integrate into new material.

In 2022, Ben and Matt launched Artists Equity, a production company aimed at sharing profits with the cast and crew. Ben was inspired by a fond memory of getting a $400 residual check for an acting job at a time when he was on the verge of bankruptcy. That small check made a big impact, and it shaped their philosophy: everyone who contributes to a production—actors, directors, prop people, cinematographers—deserves a share of the success.

Fede Álvarez

In 2024, I moderated a panel at the DGA's annual Digital Day where filmmaker Fede Álvarez took us behind the scenes of his hit movie, *Alien: Romulus*. As a huge fan of Ridley Scott's *Alien* and James Cameron's *Aliens*, Fede crafted his film to bridge the two classics. He even tracked down the original team that built the creatures of those films and assembled the artists again. I was very impressed with the reverence he showed to the two original films. The set design and graphics reflected the state of the art of the '80s, while CGI was used sparingly. Fede did everything he could practically.

To introduce Fede to the DGA audience, I showed a clip from his first short, *Panic Attack*. Back in 2009, while working in a visual effects studio in Uruguay, Fede made this low-budget sci-fi short. In it, gigantic alien robots crash through the streets of Montevideo, blasting buildings and sending people fleeing in terror. It looked like a hundred-million-dollar blockbuster. The budget was $300. The easiest way to show it to his family and friends was to post it on YouTube, which had just launched four years earlier. Little did he know it would go viral and catch the attention of Kanye West, who promoted it. That buzz eventually led to Sam Raimi hiring Fede to direct his first American feature, a remake of Raimi's 1981 horror classic, *Evil Dead*.

Fede's handling of the genre made him the right guy to direct other horror films, *Don't Breathe* and *Texas Chainsaw Massacre*.

While Ridley Scott was directing *Prometheus*, Fede pitched him a new idea for the *Alien* franchise. It wasn't until years later that Ridley called him back to start work on developing *Alien: Romulus*.

Fede's enthusiasm for his *Alien* movie is inspiring. He shared with our Digital Day crowd how excited he was to present the film to Cameron, Scott, and a preview audience. When he showed us a clip of the chestburster squirming out of a woman, I asked him if Disney executives had a problem with the creepy violence. He laughed and admitted they did, and that he would have been disappointed if they hadn't requested changes. Still, he pushed back and got an unusual number of disturbing sequences approved by Disney.

At another event, Fede casually mentioned being a professional pianist. He shrugged it off, saying, "I hate to look like I'm bragging, but there it is."

We'll be seeing a lot more movies from this likable artist.

Ken Annakin

When I interviewed British director Ken Annakin for the DGA Visual History program, he revealed that his first picture was *Breastfeeding*. A short film commissioned by the British Ministry of Information to persuade women to breastfeed their children. The purpose was to save milk during World War II.

Ken's career spanned a wide range of genres. In England, he made comedies and went on to direct several Disney family classics, including *Swiss Family Robinson*. He also helmed the hilarious big-budget adventure *Those Magnificent Men in Their Flying Machines*, filmed in the expansive 70mm Todd-AO format. But humor was just one of his many talents. On sprawling war epics like *Battle of the Bulge* and *The Longest Day*, Ken commanded the set with the precision of a seasoned general.

After our interview, I read his memoir, *So You Wanna Be a Director?* One quote particularly resonated with me: "The greatest kick in being a director is knowing that at the end of the day, you have taken a bare set and added something to it with actors which could never have existed without your imagination or the technique to make it happen. I suppose you could call them artistic orgasms."

Ken shared some colorful stories in his book. For instance, while filming *Miranda*, he recounted how Glynis Johns, who played a mermaid, tried to seduce him the night before a shoot. He declined with a reminder: "Don't forget, your call is 6:30 in makeup, and you'd better look better on the set than you do now, or I'll have to keep you in long shot. Kiss, kiss, darling!"

One of his last films was *The Pirate Movie* with my *Blue Lagoon* discovery, Christopher Atkins, playing the lead.

You can find a link to my interview with Ken at www.randalkleiser.com

Darren Aronofsky

I sketched this around the time Darren Aronofsky was promoting *Black Swan*, a film that I find both sensual and terrifying. Natalie Portman's Oscar-winning performance as a ballerina striving for perfection while descending into madness is unforgettable.

Darren has a way of pushing his actors to their limits. A prime example is the shocking climax of *Mother!* where (spoiler alert) Jennifer Lawrence's character is literally torn apart. Darren immerses the audience in his protagonist's nightmare, making it visceral and haunting.

In *The Wrestler*, Darren took audiences behind the scenes of professional wrestling, delivering an unflinching portrayal of a broken-down athlete. Mickey Rourke's performance as the aging wrestler feels raw and authentic, partly because Rourke improvised many of his scenes. His commitment was extraordinary, from actually cutting his face with a razor blade to having his flesh stapled on camera. The moments in the locker room and his playful interaction with kids showcase his talent for improvisation. Rourke's scenes with Evan Rachel Wood, who plays his estranged daughter, are heartbreakingly tender.

Darren's filmmaking style was shaped by his upbringing near Coney Island, where the Cyclone roller coaster became a metaphor for the intensity he brings to his films. He has a knack for placing the viewer directly in his protagonist's shoes to show where their mind goes. He sometimes uses a technique he calls a "hip hop montage", a rapid-fire sequence of sharp images and sounds. You can see this vividly in the addiction scenes from *Requiem for a Dream*.

Darren guided Brendan Fraser to an Academy Award for Best Actor in *The Whale*. His line, "I need to know that I've done one thing right with my life," hit me deeply, capturing Fraser's character's pain and humanity.

Darren is also a pioneer in cutting-edge technology. He became the first director to create content for the Las Vegas Sphere. His immersive project, *Postcard from Earth*, was shot in 18K and projected at 60 frames per second. Mind blowing.

Jacques Audiard

I did this sketch at the DGA "Meet the Nominees" symposium in 2025, where Jacques was up for Best Director for *Emilia Pérez*. I'm so glad I went into this film knowing nothing about it. I was swept along by the unique story of a cartel drug lord who wants to change his sex. The movie unfolds in an original way, using clever musical sequences.

When I later met Jacques and praised his staging of the numbers, he responded with, "That's quite a compliment coming from you." That gave me a nice boost.

Jacques grew up in the film industry. His father, Michel Audiard, was a successful writer-director. At 15, he announced, "I'll be in cinema if I fail at everything else." Jacques originally wanted to become a literature or philosophy professor; however, he dropped out of the Sorbonne before graduating. His entry into the industry was working as an assistant editor, and one of his first jobs was on Roman Polanski's *The Tenant*. After writing several produced screenplays, his directorial debut, *See How They Fall*, won the César Award for Best First Film.

Many of his films explore the struggle to communicate despite language barriers. In *Read My Lips*, the protagonist is deaf, and in *The Beat That My Heart Skipped*, a brutal thug who wants to become a concert pianist must learn from a teacher who doesn't speak his language. With *Dheepan*, he pushed himself further, filming in a language he didn't understand about a subject he initially knew little about: the plight of Indian refugees.

His film *Rust and Bone* stars Marion Cotillard as an orca trainer who loses her legs after an accident, and becomes entangled with an unemployed kickboxer, played by Matthias Schoenaerts. In one sensual sequence, he takes her to the beach for a swim. The visual effects to remove her legs are flawless. Another extraordinary highlight is when Marion communicates with an orca through hand signals at the big glass tank. Marion plays the whole movie without makeup and looks gorgeous. Meanwhile, Matthias has a harrowing scene where he rescues his 5-year-old son from beneath the ice of a frozen lake.

Jacques' *A Prophet* tells the gripping rise of a young Arab who works his way up in prison to top dog. The film won the Grand Prix at the Cannes Film Festival and earned an Academy Award Nomination for Best Foreign Language Film.

I love his quote, "I don't want my children to ever see me when I'm on set, because I look like a crazy man."

John Badham

John arrived in Los Angeles with two Yale degrees and began his career in the mailroom at Universal. After working his way into casting and then directing episodic television, he got his first feature assignment, *The Bingo Long Traveling All-Stars & Motor Kings*. This led to the hit *Saturday Night Fever*. His career was launched.

John's filmography is impressively diverse, covering everything from *Dracula* to *WarGames* to *Stakeout*. His action-packed *Blue Thunder* is especially notable for its daring helicopter stunts over downtown LA, accomplished without the benefit of modern computer graphics. It's worth revisiting to appreciate the unique, high-stakes stunt work.

In 2012, I invited John to be part of a summer workshop at Cal State San Bernardino, where he conducted a two-week directing course. Students from around the world converged on the campus and worked with actors under John's guidance.

I have visited John's directing class at Chapman University twice—once for a disastrous out-of-focus screening of my film *Getting It Right*. The 35mm print had been stored in my attic, causing it to warp. Despite that, John was gracious enough to invite me back when I asked to work with his students on blocking techniques for my virtual reality project, *Defrost*.

We are also linked by our association with puppeteers Tony Urbano and Tim Blaine, who did *Short Circuit* for John and *Flight of the Navigator* for me. And then there's John Travolta. At the 40th anniversary screening of *Saturday Night Fever* at the Directors Guild, I had the honor of introducing my friend, John Badham.

I highly recommend the two books he has written: *I'll Be in My Trailer: The Creative Wars Between Directors and Actors*, and *John Badham on Directing*. One of his standout pieces of advice: "If an actor comes up with a terrible idea, instead of putting it down, ask them to explain it more. 'I never saw it that way.' If you ignore them, it will come back to bite you."

Paul Bartel

At DGA meetings, Paul always kept us laughing with his warmth, wit, and mischievous sense of humor.

Originally, Paul dreamed of being an animation director, but after studying at UCLA, he realized that the kind of stylish and innovative animation he wanted to do was no longer in fashion. He pivoted to studying theater and acting in films. After receiving a Fulbright scholarship, he went to Italy to study film at Centro Sperimentale di Cinematografia. Obsessed with Italian cinema, Paul had the opportunity to attend lectures and watch rough cuts by directors like Bernardo Bertolucci. Returning to the States, he worked for a commercial company where he used their facilities to make his first short, *The Secret Cinema*, which caught the attention of Brian De Palma, who cast Paul in a role in *Hi, Mom!*

Gene Corman, Roger's brother, gave Paul his first directing assignment, *Private Parts*. Despite good reviews, newspapers refused to print the title, and MGM even took their name off the film. Paul convinced Roger Corman to give him another chance and got to direct *Death Race 2000*, for which he was paid the grand sum of $5,000.

Paul's breakout success came with *Eating Raoul*, financed largely by his supportive parents, who sold their house and cashed in their stocks to make it happen. Nice parents. They got their money back, made a profit, and helped launch their son's place in cult cinema history.

In 1984, actor/producer Tab Hunter hired Paul to direct the super campy *Lust in the Dust*. John Waters had rejected it since he hadn't written it. Joining Tab in the cast were Divine and my friend Lainie Kazan. Paul wanted to make an homage to the Sergio Leone westerns and shot the film in scope. Unfortunately, after having post problems, Tab Hunter outvoted Paul and released the movie in 1.85, making many of the stylistic closeups of eyes and guns ineffective. One print was made with substandard color but was at least in scope, and Paul got hold of it and donated it to the Museum of Modern Art.

In his interview for my documentary *Directing: How to Get There*, Paul had an unusual suggestion for up-and-coming filmmakers: "Buy a van, volunteer to help out on an independent feature, then two weeks into the shoot tell the production that you need to be paid for further use of the van."

We lost Paul in 2000 at age 61. He left a legacy of inventive, subversive films and warm memories of his charm and creativity.

Michael Bay

Michael has a knack for blowing things up, both on and off the screen. I saw him in his element during a visit to Hawaii on the set of *Pearl Harbor*. He was filming a dialogue scene with Kate Beckinsale and Ben Affleck outside a Navy location. When he spotted me, he paused production for five minutes to show me a previs video. His excitement was contagious, like a child showing off a new toy. The clip was a computer-animated rendering, capturing the point of view of a bomb falling from the sky and striking the deck of an aircraft carrier. When I saw the final shot in the movie, I was amazed to see how precisely it matched the previs. That was my introduction to a whole new approach to planning cinematic sequences.

Michael also went to great lengths to bring authenticity to *Pearl Harbor*, interviewing soldiers who had lived through the attack. He staged specific moments based on their accounts, infusing the film with a gritty realism.

I've always admired the ultra-commercial style of his large-scale action films, from *Armageddon* to *The Rock*, *The Island*, and *Ambulance*. No one creates spectacle quite like Michael Bay. Behind the chaos of his explosive set pieces is a meticulous attention to safety. He works closely with his top-notch crew to anticipate anything that could go wrong.

Michael retains the excitement of his youth. When he was a kid, he set his bedroom on fire while shooting a Super 8 movie. At fifteen, he interned for my friend George Lucas filing storyboards for *Raiders of the Lost Ark*. When he saw the completed film, he was hooked on directing, a passion so intense that, even today, he never leaves the set during production.

Over the years, Michael has become a genre unto himself, his films often referred to as "Bayhem." There's no doubt he'll go down in history as one of cinema's most influential action directors.

Warren Beatty

In 1977, during pre-production for *Grease*, I was walking across the Paramount lot when I saw a group of football players heading my way. Mistaking one of them for a friend, I called out, "What are you doing here?" To my surprise, the man shot back, "What are YOU doing here?" As he passed, I realized my "friend" was none other than Warren Beatty. He was on the lot directing his first feature, *Heaven Can Wait*. I'm sure he thought I was just a crazy fan.

Later, during our rehearsals for *Grease* on a soundstage, both Warren and Jack Nicholson, working in nearby offices, complained that they couldn't concentrate because of the noise. Oops!

Warren's next directing project was *Reds*, a sweeping, controversial 3-hour and 15-minute epic that he also produced, wrote, and starred in. The film grossed $40 million and earned 12 Oscar nominations. Warren won the Academy Award for Best Director, and my dear friend Maureen Stapleton took home Best Supporting Actress. She told me an anecdote about enduring 80 takes of a single scene. Fed up, she quipped to Warren, "Are you out of your fucking mind?" The crew erupted in applause.

Warren's next directing job was a complete change of pace, *Dick Tracy*, where he guided Al Pacino to play one of the most over-the-top, campy performances I've ever seen, the villainous Big Boy Caprice.

Warren has had an amazing career, from movie star to Oscar-winning director. Along the way, he became a mentor to others. Robert Downey Jr. once shared how Warren grilled him on his character's action in a scene—a technique he credited to Warren's acting teacher, Stella Adler.

Warren is the only person to be nominated for acting, directing, writing, and producing the same film, achieving this feat with both *Heaven Can Wait* and *Reds*. Over his career, his films have earned 53 Academy Award nominations.

Warren Beatty isn't just a star and filmmaker; he's a true Hollywood icon.

Robert Benton

"Hire the best people and listen wisely." "Directing is time management." "90 percent of directing is damage control." "Don't make the same mistake twice...Don't make it a third time." These are all great tips I've tried to follow from writer-director Robert Benton.

Growing up with severe dyslexia, Robert struggled with reading, spelling, and punctuation. Amazingly, he went on to earn three Oscar nominations for his writing for *Bonnie and Clyde*, *The Late Show*, and *Nobody's Fool*, and took home two Academy Awards for the screenplays of *Places in the Heart* and *Kramer vs. Kramer*. He also won a third one for directing the latter. And he co-wrote the 1978 movie, *Superman*.

Robert learned everything about storytelling from watching movies over and over. He saw *A Place in the Sun* more than ten times and began to understand how stories are structured. For him, *Chinatown* and *The Godfather: Part II* are perfect scripts, while *Singin' in the Rain* is a perfect work of art.

Robert and I share a deep admiration for the late cinematographer Néstor Almendros, whose artistry elevated every project he touched. They collaborated on five movies, including his Oscar winners, *Kramer vs. Kramer* and *Places in the Heart*. My friends, editor Carol Littleton and cinematographer John Bailey, drew my attention to a particularly moving scene in *Places in the Heart*. At the end of the movie, a collection plate is passed from one churchgoer to another in an uninterrupted shot, with the camera moving slowly forward. Carol explained that Néstor had grips move the pews out of the way during the take. As the collection plate reaches the back row, we see two characters who died earlier in the film. This surprise packed an emotional wallop.

Robert and I once discussed how Néstor would choose a painter's visual style to emulate for each film. In his book *A Man with a Camera*, Néstor wrote a chapter on each movie and detailed his experiences with the different directors. I am very proud that he included a chapter on my movie, *The Blue Lagoon*.

Néstor was the best artist and human being I was lucky enough to work with, and Robert shares the same reputation. Known for his sensitivity and laid-back style, he brings out the best in everyone on set.

"What I want is to make movies end five minutes before the audience wants them to end."

Kathryn Bigelow

Kathryn and I have crossed paths many times over the years, and she never ceases to surprise me. Meeting her, you'd never guess she's the force behind some of cinema's most intense and violent action films. She comes across as sharp, effortlessly cool, and more like someone who belongs in front of the camera than behind it.

Originally, Kathryn aspired to be an artist and studied painting. Her path shifted dramatically when she made her first short film, *The Set-Up*, while studying under Miloš Forman at Columbia University. It was the beginning of her exploration of cinematic violence. She instructed the two actors to actually beat each other up on camera. This was the end of painting because she found cinema was too seductive to resist.

Kathryn redefined the cop genre with *Blue Steel*, casting Jamie Lee Curtis as a tough, action lead. She delivered a wild blend of genres in *Near Dark*, a vampire western romance dark comedy horror (yes, all of those) starring Bill Paxton and Lance Henriksen in unforgettable roles. Then came *Point Break*, where Kathryn turned extreme athletes into memorable robber-killers and created the very cool duo of Keanu Reeves and Patrick Swayze.

I recently rewatched her exciting movie *Strange Days*, from 1995, and was struck by how ahead of its time it was in predicting the specifics of virtual reality. By using a wide-angle lens and filming from the viewer's point of view, Kathryn simulated the experience of wearing a VR headset almost two decades before they were released to the public. To achieve this, her team developed an eight-pound camera to do the incredible opening sequence where the viewer (spoiler alert!) jumps off a roof.

Kathryn later transitioned from pop culture blockbusters to politically charged films, while retaining her visceral style. In 2010, she made history as the first woman to win the Academy Award for Best Director for *The Hurt Locker*. Her *A House of Dynamite* is a chilling reminder of what could happen and who has their finger on the red button.

Kathryn and I have worked together on the Directors Guild Special Projects Committee, where our goal is to prepare our members for the technological changes of the future. She has experimented with shooting content on the iPhone and finds it nimble and malleable, making the filming process much less apprehensive. I have no doubt that she will continue to dazzle us by using cutting-edge tech in bold and compelling ways.

Peter Bogdanovich

Peter first caught my attention with his debut film, *Targets*, which featured my childhood favorite actor, Boris Karloff. Roger Corman had given Peter a unique challenge: if he could devise a way to shoot a film using Karloff for only two days, he'd greenlight the project. Rising to the occasion, Peter created a story about a mass shooter who hides behind a drive-in movie screen, targeting the audience in their cars. The film includes an ironic and clever scene where Karloff's character makes a personal appearance at the drive-in. The shooter sees him and is frightened away.

My favorite of Peter's films is *Paper Moon*, featuring Tatum O'Neal's Oscar-winning performance. Peter said he learned the grammar of cinema by immersing himself in countless classic films. He once had a conversation with Howard Hawks about *What's Up, Doc?*, where he admitted borrowing heavily from Hawks' *Bringing Up Baby*. Hawks didn't mind, quipping, "Just don't make it cute," and confessing he'd borrowed plenty of ideas himself.

Before becoming an Oscar-nominated director, Peter studied acting under Stella Adler, gaining a deep appreciation for performance. Alongside his directing career, he was a respected film historian, writing insightful monographs for the Museum of Modern Art on cinematic legends like Hawks, Hitchcock, and Ford. He also created the definitive documentary on Buster Keaton, *The Great Buster.*

Peter observed that directors often resembled their films: John Ford, a six-time Oscar winner, was as gruff as his Westerns, though Peter recalled catching the occasional smile during their conversations.

Peter's relationship with Orson Welles was professional and personal. He wrote extensively about Welles, conducted numerous interviews, and even invited Welles to live in his home—a stay that stretched over several years.

I often saw Peter at Henry Jaglom's New Year's Eve parties. Both appeared in Orson Welles' *The Other Side of the Wind*, which Peter finished after Orson's death. Peter and Henry both wrote books about Orson and had an ongoing argument over who was closer to him.

Peter once said he had one foot in the Old Hollywood, which he loved, and one foot in the New Hollywood, which he was part of, but wasn't interested in. His voice was a bridge between eras.

Mel Brooks

"It's good to be the king."

Where do I start with Mel Brooks? I've admired him all my life. I have watched two of his films over and over... *Young Frankenstein* ("Frau Blücher" [horses whinny]) and *High Anxiety* (Madeline Kahn's erotic phone call and the zany airport security sequence). Mel said that Madeline was the single best comedienne who ever lived, and I have to agree. Her character Lily von Shtüpp, a parody of Marlene Dietrich in *Blazing Saddles*, is side-splittingly funny. (It was a thrill to direct her in an episode of *New York News*.)

Mel is a genius, known for trusting his instincts even when faced with resistance. He famously fought for *Blazing Saddles'* hysterical fart scene and the controversial "Springtime for Hitler" musical number in *The Producers*. Mel consistently pushes boundaries, never shying away from the outrageous or the audacious.

In *History of the World, Part I*, Mel cast himself as a waiter at The Last Supper, asking, "Separate checks?" As Moses, he dropped the 15 commandments, leaving 10.

While known for his laugh-out-loud comedies, Mel also produced classy movies like *The Elephant Man* and *84 Charing Cross Road*. You'd never imagine Mel was the producer of the horror film *The Fly*, in which Jeff Goldblum delivered a creepy, unforgettable performance. My good friend Jonathan Sanger, who produced several movies for him, told me Mel never puts his name on dramatic films to avoid confusing his audience—they know him for broad comedy.

Mel's personal life had a similar contrast; he was married to the award-winning dramatic actress Anne Bancroft. Their chemistry is evident in vintage TV appearances where Mel's quick wit and Anne's poise made them the perfect pair.

Regarding comedy, he once said, "Tragedy is when I cut my finger. Comedy is when you walk into an open sewer and die. But seriously, folks, humor is the conscience of mankind."

In recent years, Mel carried on his comedy legacy by producing *History of the World, Part II*, and passing the directing torch to his protégés.

I was thrilled to meet Mel at a memorial tribute to his frequent collaborator Gene Wilder, where I photographed him with Gene's co-star in *The Woman in Red*, Kelly LeBrock.

James Burrows

Jim's connection to classic television is legendary, with credits on iconic shows like *The Mary Tyler Moore Show, The Bob Newhart Show, Laverne & Shirley, Lou Grant*, and *Rhoda*, among others. Comedy was in his blood, inherited from his father, Broadway writer Abe Burrows. Abe had a unique method: by listening to actors backstage, he could tell if scenes were landing based on their rhythm—an insight Jim carried with him throughout his career.

My friend Joel Thurm told me about Jim's early days in LA when he was trying to break into half-hour sitcoms. Joel played a pivotal role in launching his career by reminding Jim about his connection to Mary Tyler Moore. Years earlier, as the second assistant stage manager on the ill-fated Broadway production *Breakfast at Tiffany's*, Jim's job was to escort Mary to and from the set and look out for her. Joel suggested Jim write a letter to Mary's husband, producer Grant Tinker. The gamble paid off. Soon, Jim was directing episodes of *The Mary Tyler Moore Show*, which opened doors to his career-defining work, including the pilot episode of *Taxi*, his favorite project.

As casting director, Joel brought in Danny DeVito for his first major TV role, the pilot episode of *Taxi*. Jim decided to give Danny a memorable introduction: his character barks orders from a lofty office—until he steps out. The sight gag was an instant hit.

Jim went on to direct 75 episodes of *Taxi*, 237 episodes of *Cheers*, and 32 episodes of *Frasier*. And he hasn't slowed down, adding hit shows like *Friends* and many others to his lengthy resume.

He was initially concerned about the gay material in *Will & Grace*, knowing that 25 percent of the country might not tune in. But he was flattered when President Joe Biden told him how the show helped soften much of America's resistance to gay representation on television. He continued the trend with the series *Mid Century Modern* starring the wonderful Nathan Lane.

Here's a fun fact: if you play all of Jim's content consecutively, 24/7, it would take over two weeks to watch. With eleven Emmys to his name, Jim Burrows will go down as one of the biggest names in television history.

Gil Cates

Gil was one of the most respected and well-liked figures in the film industry. He produced the Academy Awards fourteen times and founded and directed the Geffen Playhouse and the UCLA School of Theater, Film, and Television. He also served as president of the Directors Guild for two terms and continued to fight for directors' creative rights until his passing in 2011.

My favorite movie he directed was the emotional drama *I Never Sang for My Father*. Rewatching it recently, I was struck by several memorable moments. In one scene, Gene Hackman, playing a college professor, walks through a nursing home that he is considering for his father. An ominous score plays as images of the feeble residents eating soup are intercut with shots of his strong father, Melvyn Douglas, doing the same. The juxtaposition is haunting. In another heartbreaking scene, the father lashes out at his children, denying his declining competence. Just before storming off, there's a fleeting, poignant moment when he realizes they might be right. And the brutal father-son argument between Gene Hackman and Melvyn Douglas at the end is gut-wrenching. Gil's direction brought out some of the most moving work of Melvyn Douglas' career.

I had the privilege of working with Douglas on my short film, *Portrait of Grandpa Doc*, where he played my grandfather with warmth and nuance. It was a similar character to his role in *I Never Sang for My Father*, yet completely opposite in demeanor. A testament to his remarkable range as an actor.

Gil once described directing feature films as akin to oil painting, where you have the luxury of time to perfect your work, while shooting for television was like creating a watercolor, requiring quick decisions and living with the results.

In his youth, Gil faced overt anti-Semitism and changed his name from Katz to Cates. His legacy lives on through his son, Gil Cates Jr., who has directed several features and now runs the Geffen Playhouse. Both father and son were longtime members of the Western Directors Council, guiding many of the Guild's key decisions.

In an industry where true gentlemen are rare, Gil and his son stand out as class acts.

Jeremiah Chechik

Jeremiah and I often cross paths at Political Action Committee meetings at the DGA, where U.S. senators and members of Congress join us to discuss runaway production, piracy, copyright infringement, and safeguarding First Amendment freedoms.

Jeremiah's career began in Toronto as a photographer before he transitioned to shooting fashion spreads for Italian Vogue. This opened the door to commercial work, including a memorable shoot where he filmed a girl sipping wine. After 50 takes, he quipped, "Print number one and fifty."

Once, during a flight, Jeremiah read an article about Stanley Kubrick, who mentioned admiring a series of Michelob commercials. Jeremiah was floored—those commercials were his.

His first Hollywood feature was *National Lampoon's Christmas Vacation*. Initially hesitant about directing the third in the series, Jeremiah wasn't sure why Chevy Chase had asked for him—his commercials were moody and artsy, not comedic. But the two hit it off, and Jeremiah decided not to watch the previous films to ensure his take was unique. The result? A holiday classic and a box office hit.

A longtime fan of the TV show *The Avengers*, Jeremiah jumped at the chance to direct its feature adaptation with Sean Connery. Although initially intimidated, he found Connery professional and engaged, driving himself to set, knowing his lines, and taking direction well. However, Connery was quick to voice his displeasure when kept waiting, directing his frustration at the AD, but never at Jeremiah.

In his remake of the French thriller *Diabolique*, Jeremiah elicited an illicitly sexy performance from Sharon Stone playing the femme fatale, with characters being apparently killed and coming back unexpectedly in the style of thrillers of the '90s.

Jeremiah was hired to direct *Honey, I Blew Up the Kid*, but creative and budget differences caused him to split with Disney. Jeff Katzenberg asked me to step in and take over with the promise of an adult-themed movie right after. Jeremiah had conceived an army of ice cream trucks leading the giant baby out of Vegas…I changed it to one truck. He designed a huge lab for Rick Moranis' character to work in…I kept the design, but cut the set in half and only shot one side of it. Disney got their cost-effective version, and Jeff Katzenberg moved to DreamWorks. I got… well, let's just say I'm still waiting for that adult-themed movie.

Michael Cimino

Michael Cimino studied painting and architecture at Yale. After graduation, he moved to New York and began directing commercials. He ventured into screenwriting, and his script *Thunderbolt and Lightfoot* caught the attention of Clint Eastwood, the biggest movie star in the world at the time. In a Rocky-style move, Cimino refused to sell the script unless he could direct it. Eastwood took a gamble, offering him a key piece of advice: "Mike, you have to will things through."

Michael's lack of traditional training led him to create his own methods. He claimed he could make any movie with just a 250mm zoom lens and a 30mm lens. He also dismissed storyboards as tools for directors who "can't see," likening them to painting by numbers. He described himself as "not a teacher, not a preacher, but a reacher."

Michael had major success with *The Deer Hunter*. The Russian roulette sequences with Christopher Walken and Robert De Niro are burned in my memory. His childhood idol, John Wayne, handed him the Best Director Oscar for that film.

In Hollywood, when you're hot, you're hot, and Michael was given free rein by United Artists to make *Heaven's Gate*. With unlimited studio support, he indulged himself: waiting hours for the perfect cloud formations, ripping out a street to widen the sidewalks, and going many months over schedule. His perfectionism almost bankrupted the studio, and he became the poster child for out-of-control filmmakers. The media tore him apart, and the film's failure ended Hollywood's auteur period of the '70s.

Cimino directed *Year of the Dragon*, which failed to bring him the comeback he hoped for. I admired the scale and scope of *The Sicilian*, but once again, Cimino went over schedule and budget. By 1996, he had retired from filmmaking.

Time can change how a movie is perceived. In 2012, a re-edited version of *Heaven's Gate* was shown at the Venice Film Festival, where Michael received a standing ovation. Quoting Count Basie, he said: "It's not how you handle the hills, it's how you handle the valleys."

I had seen photos of him early in his career, looking like a typical New York Italian. He went through a reclusive period where he lost weight and had plastic surgery. I wasn't prepared for the striking transition when I ran into him at a party in 2015.

Roman Coppola

Being the son of a legendary director like Francis Ford Coppola comes with its own mix of privileges and challenges. Roman grew up with a front-row seat to cinematic history, taking on roles as an actor, visual effects consultant, second unit director, and president of American Zoetrope. He associates his childhood milestones with his father's films—third grade with *The Godfather Part II*, and sixth grade with *Apocalypse Now*.

Despite the shadow of his family name, Roman managed to carve his own path, earning an Oscar nomination for co-writing the screenplay for *Moonrise Kingdom* with Wes Anderson. Their creative partnership continued with *The French Dispatch*, *Asteroid City*, and *The Phoenician Scheme*.

Roman's feature directing debut, *CQ*, was a love letter to the '70s film industry, inspired by his own childhood memories. The story follows a young film editor working on a Barbarella-type movie and boasts an impressive cast: Giancarlo Giannini, Gérard Depardieu, and John Phillip Law in his final film appearance.

Roman has also made his mark in television, creating the offbeat series *Mozart in the Jungle*, starring Gael García Bernal. Based loosely on the life of conductor Gustavo Dudamel, the show explored the quirky, passionate world of classical music.

Roman has directed music videos for groups like Daft Punk and Green Day, but perhaps the cleverest is one he did for Phoenix entitled "Funky Squaredance". Since the band had no budget, Roman took the song and concocted a stream of consciousness texts and random images. The video was invited into the permanent collection at the New York Museum of Modern Art.

In 2024, Roman started the magazine Enthousiasmos with Johan Chiaramonte. Its tagline, "for the curious enthusiast," says it all. The first issue featured Luca Guadagnino on the cover, with an interview designed to feel like having a meal with someone and sharing a deep dive into mutual experiences.

Roman believes the most important trait for a director is good taste. "Look at A Simple Man by Tom Ford," he says, "Tom is a fashion designer and was able to make his first film with great style and success."

Brady Corbet

Brady grew up in the small town of Glenwood Springs, Colorado, and was a cineast as far back as he can remember. One of his favorite films was *Metropolis*. His acting career began at seven. Thanks in part to his hometown of just ten thousand people serving as a national casting hub. His grandfather spotted an ad and encouraged him to apply. By age eleven, Brady landed a role on the popular TV show *The King of Queens*.

Years of acting gave him a front-row seat to the work of many directors—including Lars von Trier and Michael Haneke—he quickly realized that directing a movie was like "herding cats and spinning plates." He was hooked.

At twenty-six, Brady made his directorial debut with *The Childhood of a Leader*, a haunting period drama set in post-World War I France. Loosely inspired by the homonymous Jean-Paul Sartre short story, the film explores how childhood experiences can shape the rise of a future dictator.

His second feature, *Vox Lux*, was partly a reaction to the Columbine shooting. It tells the story of a young girl whose traumatic experience catapults her into pop stardom, and examines how the costs of fame can even be handed down to her daughter.

For his 1950s epic, *The Brutalist*, Brady turned his attention to the complex dynamic between an artist and a patron who doesn't share his ideals. "You often end up in bed with people with less morals and ethics than you, and you need to protect the flame of your project from burning out." Determined to capture his protagonist's architectural vision accurately, he chose to shoot in VistaVision, a large format that avoided the distortion common to standard 35mm. The shoot was as brutal as the title suggests. Directing seven pages a day, Brady even spent part of the time hooked up to an IV bag, carried around by an assistant. "There's a lot in common between constructing a building and making a movie. It requires roughly the same amount of personnel, depending on the project." Remarkably, he turned a ten-million-dollar budget into a film that looks ten times that amount. With a runtime of three and a half hours, Brady added an intermission to ensure the audience wouldn't be preoccupied with bathroom breaks during the second half. The film earned widespread acclaim, and Brady won Best Director at the 82nd Golden Globe Awards.

"Fame is one of the potential hazards of this job, but I really just want to make movies. I want to be respected, sure. But famous-famous? If you don't care about that stuff, you really are free."

Costa-Gavras

Costa-Gavras directed two of my favorite political thrillers, *Z* and *Missing*. Both films feel like gritty documentaries. *Z* won the Academy Award for Best Foreign Language Film and *Missing*, the Palme d'Or.

When Konstantinos "Kostas" Gavras made his first movie, a typo in the credits changed his name to Costa-Gavras. Fixing the error was too costly, so he adopted the new name. Actress Simone Signoret told him it sounded very French, and he decided to keep it.

Widely regarded as a master of political cinema, Costa-Gavras doesn't shy away from controversial topics: *State of Siege* examines the dictatorship in Uruguay, *Betrayed* delves into neo-Nazism in America, *Music Box* follows the trial of a man accused of leading a death squad, and *Amen* critiques the Pope's silence during the Holocaust.

In 1982, he was asked to take over the Cinémathèque Française, and he turned it down, thinking it was a lot of work with no pay. When President Mitterrand personally requested it, he gave in and accepted. During his first five-year term, he invited American directors like Bob Fosse and Henry Hathaway to France to be honored, along with legendary actors like Bette Davis, who was a huge hit. He programmed the showing of silent films with accompanying music and oversaw the preservation of over 25,000 prints, transferring nitrate prints to safer formats.

In 2009, I was in Paris when Costa-Gavras hosted a screening of Pierrot le Fou with Jean-Paul Belmondo as a featured guest. My friend Jacques Fieschi had a ticket he couldn't use, so I went, expecting to know no one. To my surprise, many French directors greeted me—they had attended the annual lunches I hosted for twenty years for the French festival at the DGA. Costa-Gavras conducted an amazing interview with Belmondo and, to top it off, I was seated next to Jean-Pierre Léaud from Truffaut's *The 400 Blows*. A truly unforgettable evening.

In 2003, John Landis conducted a fascinating DGA Visual History interview where Costa-Gavras said, "When I go to a movie, I say, 'I'm yours. Tell me anything you want, I'll believe you for the first ten minutes. But then, if it's not good, I say, 'Hey, you are manipulating me or cheating me.' It's so easy to manipulate. We have to be honest with audiences."

Kevin Costner

I've always been a big admirer of Kevin Costner. The first time I met him was in the early 1980s at the launch party for photographer Greg Gorman's studio. Kevin was casually hanging out in the kitchen, laid-back, friendly, and approachable. Coming from a blue-collar family, Kevin never envisioned a career in acting; it wasn't even on his radar. He stumbled into it during college and got hooked.

Early in his career, he filmed several scenes for *The Big Chill*, but director Lawrence Kasdan ended up cutting them. True to his word, though, Kasdan promised Kevin a role in a future project, which turned out to be *Silverado*. Watching him ride a horse bareback up onto a wooden porch inspired me to learn how to ride my horse without a saddle. It's a great connective experience because it causes you to think like a horse and look ahead for any distractions.

Silverado launched his successful acting career, playing the leads in *The Untouchables, No Way Out, Bull Durham, Field of Dreams, JFK, Robin Hood: Prince of Thieves, The Bodyguard*, and the hit series *Yellowstone*.

From a directing standpoint, my favorite film of his, *Dances with Wolves*, was a critical and box office hit. Kevin plays a Union Army Lieutenant who gets involved with a group of Lakota Indians. Much of the dialogue is in Lakota with English subtitles. While recording John Barry's score, Kevin asked if he could speak to the orchestra. He wanted to tell them the story and how much it meant to him. Then, he requested to play the kettle drum on one of the cues. John Barry and the musicians were amused to see the director energetically pounding the drum. The film won seven Academy Awards, including Best Picture and Best Director.

But even a career like Kevin's isn't immune to setbacks. After the success of *Dances with Wolves*, he directed *The Postman*, a post-apocalyptic action-adventure that "won" five Golden Raspberry Awards. Undeterred, Kevin re-launched his directorial career with *Open Range*. He invested a million dollars to build a town from scratch and an additional $40,000 to construct a road just to get to it. The effort paid off with a film praised for its historical authenticity and Robert Duvall's performance. It features the longest shootout I've seen in the Western genre.

Twenty years later, Kevin launched *Horizon: An American Saga* as an ambitious four-part film series.

With his long and varied career filled with many challenges, Kevin has somehow been able to retain a romantic view of Hollywood.

George Cukor

George Cukor is celebrated as the director of *My Fair Lady*, *Gaslight*, and *The Philadelphia Story*. Known for his elegance and sophistication, he also directed *The Women* but bristled at being labeled a "woman's director." His Beverly Hills mansion became a hub for the era's brightest stars, including Humphrey Bogart, Joan Crawford, Laurence Olivier, and Greta Garbo. In 1954, he directed Judy Garland and James Mason in the iconic *A Star Is Born*.

I first encountered George when he was organizing a tribute to Mae West at USC. Volunteering to assist, I was tasked with raising Miss West's microphone stand when she stood to sing. Awestruck by her presence, I missed my cue, causing an ear-piercing feedback. George graciously forgave me and later invited me to his opulent home for dinner with Miss West herself. Among the other guests were director John Schlesinger and his boyfriend, my friend, UCLA student Michael Childers. Since the mid-1930s, George was considered the unofficial head of Hollywood's gay subculture.

Over the years, I was fortunate to share many dinners at his home. Hoping to impress him, I invited George to the school carnival set of *Grease*. I seated him in a director's chair at the end of the football field and staged a full rehearsal of "We Go Together" for his enjoyment. Two hundred cast members and dancers performed in the blazing sun, lip-syncing to the playback—no cameras rolling. At the end, they all landed at his feet while George, casually eating an ice cream, turned to me and said, "Very spirited." Thinking back, I can't believe I did this. No cameras rolling??

George once took me backstage at the Ahmanson Theatre to meet his longtime friend Katharine Hepburn. Later, when I donated a bronze plaque in his honor to USC's film school, I invited Miss Hepburn to the dedication. She called my office to decline, but when I picked up the phone, I mistook her for an actor friend impersonating her. An embarrassing moment I'll never forget.

George invited me to appear in a party scene in his final movie, *Rich and Famous*. He was a good friend and confidant. When Ray Stark fired me from *Annie*, I went to George. He commiserated, sharing with me how he was replaced on *Gone With the Wind*. I felt better.

Joe Dante

Joe and I share a lot in common: a love for horror films, childhood dreams of becoming cartoonists, and time spent in art school. Our early education in filmmaking came from devouring the magazine *Famous Monsters of Filmland*. After editing trailers for Roger Corman, Joe was given the opportunity to direct *Piranha*, a riff on *Jaws*. Universal initially tried to block the release, but Steven Spielberg saw the film and admired its balance of horror and campy humor. He called off Universal's lawyers, and the movie was released. The film's success marked the start of Joe's directing career and led to his cult werewolf movie, *The Howling*.

Spielberg, recognizing Joe's knack for blending scares with laughs, hired him to direct *Gremlins*. Originally conceived as a straightforward horror film, Joe infused the project with humor, bringing the lovable Gizmo and his mischievous offspring to life. Spielberg helped shape the film's tone and creature designs, resulting in a cult classic. Joe's efforts earned him the Best Director award from the Academy of Science Fiction, Fantasy & Horror Films.

Joe paid tribute to the B-movie maestro William Castle with *Matinee*. John Goodman stars as a Castle-inspired filmmaker whose in-theater gimmicks—vibrating seats and skeletons on wires—capture the spirit of mid-century movie showmanship.

In *Innerspace*, Joe transformed a serious spy script into a surreal comedy. He pondered what it would be like if Dean Martin were miniaturized and injected into Jerry Lewis' body. That concept gave him the idea to cast Dennis Quaid and the hilarious Martin Short. The result was a hit, earning the Oscar for Best Visual Effects.

Joe's *Explorers* became one of the quintessential '80s kid-meets-alien movies that developed a devoted cult following. It also marked the debut of Ethan Hawke and River Phoenix.

In 2012, I invited Joe to participate in a Summer International Digital Cinema Workshop at Cal State San Bernardino, where students from around the world gathered to learn from industry professionals. Joe captivated the room with amusing Hollywood war stories, each one perfectly illustrating a point about the art—and chaos—of filmmaking.

Jonathan Dayton & Valerie Faris

I can always spot these two in a crowd thanks to Jonathan's signature hat. They met in 1979 at my crosstown rival school, UCLA, and started working together soon after, crafting music videos for bands like Oasis, Red Hot Chili Peppers, Beastie Boys, and The Smashing Pumpkins.

This sketch was done at the DGA "Meet the Nominees" symposium, where they discussed their breakout hit *Little Miss Sunshine*. They got good comedy performances from one of the best casts assembled for a quirky independent: Steve Carell, Toni Collette, Greg Kinnear, and Alan Arkin all shine. The film premiered at Sundance in 2006 and was picked up in one of the festival's biggest distribution deals. My friend Ron Yerxa, who served as an executive on a movie I directed, *Grandview, USA*, also produced this film.

Little Miss Sunshine received four Oscar nominations, including Best Picture, and won Best Screenplay and Best Supporting Actor for Alan Arkin, in one of his most unfiltered performances. After its success, they continued exploring relationship dynamics with the comedy *Ruby Sparks*, teaming up with Zoe Kazan—the granddaughter of the great Elia Kazan—who wrote the screenplay and starred as the title character.

Their next feature, *Battle of the Sexes*, reunited them with Steve Carell and brought Emma Stone to the fold. Both stars earned Golden Globe nominations, with Stone shining as Billie Jean King and Carell bringing humor and depth to Bobby Riggs. Billie Jean King was deeply involved in the script's development but stayed off-set to help Stone feel comfortable portraying her.

Jonathan and Valerie also directed the sharp and funny TV miniseries *Fleishman Is in Trouble*, starring Jesse Eisenberg and Claire Danes. The show followed a doctor navigating New York's online dating scene after separating from his wife.

They continue expanding their creative reach, developing new projects like *Stick* with Owen Wilson and directing commercials for high-profile clients such as Target and Pfizer.

As a husband-and-wife directing team, they admit that the line between personal and professional life can blur. Their discussions about a scene occasionally spilled into family car rides, and when their children asked if they were fighting, they'd reply they were just "discussing." Their secret? Finding projects they're passionate about and working with a cast they truly love.

Cecil B. DeMille

This is the only sketch of a director I did not actually meet or see personally. I did this from memory. When I was ten years old, my father took me to the Boyd Theatre on Chestnut Street in Philadelphia. On the screen, before the movie began, a man who looked like my grandfather stepped out from behind the curtain and addressed the audience in a theatrical mid-Atlantic accent. "Ladies and Gentlemen, young and old, this may seem an unusual procedure, speaking to you before the picture begins, but we have an unusual subject; the story of the birth of freedom. The story of Moses." I thought to myself, "Who is this guy?" He went on to explain the film's theme, then went back behind the curtain.

The Ten Commandments began to screen, and I was mesmerized by the clear storytelling, the colorful pageantry, the rousing score, and, most of all, the spectacular opening of the Red Sea. Even as a ten-year-old, I could see the matte lines and knew there was some kind of trick photography involved, but I was hooked. I began to understand what a director was and what they could do.

The practical effects stand up even today—the green mist that moves through the streets bringing death to all the firstborn males. The water turning into blood was also done very well.

My admiration for Cecil B. DeMille grew when I watched *Samson and Delilah* and saw the temple collapse in spectacular fashion. As a kid, those larger-than-life moments left an indelible impression. Today, in an era overflowing with visual effects, I sometimes wonder if anything can truly astonish young filmgoers. But back then, I wanted to grow up and be Cecil B. DeMille.

When I arrived at USC my freshman year, I was thrilled to discover that Nina Foch, who played Moses' mother, was teaching drama there. I took her class and befriended her. Our association lasted over forty years. She told me how she once stood up to DeMille and even convinced him to shoot a line reading her way.

My one taste of the DeMille spectacle came while filming Disney's *Honey, I Blew Up the Kid* in downtown Las Vegas. Sitting on a camera crane high above the street, I watched a thousand extras below, screaming and running in a panic. They were escaping from two huge mockups of a kid's legs with tennis shoes, each the size of a bus, puppeteered by construction cranes. So fun.

Brian De Palma

"Say hello to my little friend."

This line from Brian's *Scarface* is delightfully over the top—just like much of the film, which I've watched countless times.

Brian's films swing between commercial mainstream and violent psychological thrillers, often paying homage to Hitchcock. *Body Double* is a clear nod to *Rear Window*, and *Obsession* draws heavily from *Vertigo*.

Beyond Hitchcock, he also borrowed from Eisenstein. *The Untouchables* famously recreates the Odessa Steps sequence from *Battleship Potemkin*, with a baby carriage bouncing down a staircase during a violent shootout. He guided Sean Connery to an Oscar-winning performance in that film.

Two of Brian's signature techniques are split screens and diopter shots, where the foreground and background remain in sharp focus.

His first major success was the cult classic *Carrie*. The ending scene with the hand coming out of the grave started a trend of shock twist endings in horror films. Sissy Spacek and Piper Laurie both earned Oscar nominations for their performances. At the premiere, I was surprised to see John Travolta in the audience sitting with Diana Hyland—I had just cast her as his mother in *The Boy in the Plastic Bubble* and had no idea they were dating.

At one point, Brian was interested in directing the movie *Cruising*, about a detective infiltrating the world of gay sadomasochism. William Friedkin ended up making that movie, but there is an interesting hangover in Brian's *Dressed to Kill*. The sequence where Angie Dickinson cruises a man in the Museum of Modern Art feels almost like a gay pickup encounter.

I admire his long take at the beginning of *Snake Eyes*. Other favorites are *Carlito's Way*, his second collaboration with Al Pacino, and *Casualties of War*, with its brutally realistic gang rape during the Vietnam War.

Brian was a huge admirer of Jean-Luc Godard, so it must have been a real thrill when Rolling Stone quoted Godard in 1980, praising the slow-motion sequence in *The Fury* as a standout and not a gadget.

It's surprising to learn that Brian has been nominated five times for Worst Director by the Razzies—especially considering that *Scarface*, one of his most famous films, was among them. Yet, despite the occasional critical backlash, he remains deeply admired by audiences and filmmakers alike. Love him or hate him, his influence is undeniable.

Howard Deutch

Howard Deutch's career began with a bit of family connection. His father worked at United Artists and got him a job as a trainee in the advertising and publicity department. Howard climbed the ranks to head of the department, creating trailers. He then partnered with Jeff Kanew, known as the King of Trailers, to form their own company. This gave Howard invaluable exposure to the editing styles and storytelling sensibilities of legendary directors like Martin Scorsese and Francis Ford Coppola.

When a music video was needed for Stewart Copeland and Stan Ridgway's song "Don't Box Me In" from *Rumble Fish*, Howard seized the opportunity, launching a successful run directing music videos, including Billy Joel's "Keeping the Faith" and Billy Idol's "Flesh for Fantasy." To sharpen his skills, Howard studied acting under Milton Katselas, an experience he strongly recommends for all directors. The insight gained from acting shaped his understanding of performance and storytelling.

While working on the trailer for *Sixteen Candles*, Howard crossed paths with John Hughes. Hughes, who also had an advertising background, saw a kindred spirit in Howard—another outsider in Hollywood. That connection led to Howard's first directing job: *Pretty in Pink*, featuring the Brat Pack, and launching his career. Hughes was so impressed that he offered Howard *Some Kind of Wonderful* next, where Howard met his future wife, Lea Thompson.

Next came *The Great Outdoors* starring John Candy and Dan Aykroyd, a production filled with challenges, including an unexpected snowfall during a water skiing sequence and working with Bart the Bear. Having directed Bart myself on *White Fang*, I can attest to the nerve-wracking experience of directing actors in close proximity to the enormous Kodiak bear.

Howard also ventured into horror, directing episodes of *American Horror Story*, *Tales from the Crypt*, and *True Blood*. His favorite feature? *Grumpier Old Men*, where he worked with Jack Lemmon and Walter Matthau. The film reunited these two legends for another round of bickering, insults, and late-in-life romance, with Sophia Loren joining the cast.

Howard also directed the pilot episode of *Melrose Place*. I remember reading the script and passing on it because it didn't seem to have much of a plot—just introductions to a bunch of characters. Little did I know that was the whole idea. And even less did I know that the pilot director gets paid for every subsequent episode. The show lasted for seven seasons. Lucky Howard.

Stanley Donen

I've always loved Stanley Donen's classic musical *Singin' in the Rain*. It's hard to believe that Gene Kelly pulled off his iconic dance number in the downpour while running a 101-degree fever. The film rightfully lands on countless "greatest of all time" lists.

Another favorite of mine is *On the Town*, notable for Donen's groundbreaking decision to stage elaborate musical numbers on location in the bustling streets of New York City—a rarity for its time.

One of my earliest moviegoing memories is seeing *Funny Face* when I was 11. I'll never forget the scene where Audrey Hepburn brilliantly parodies modern dance in a Parisian beatnik bar, all while Fred Astaire looks on, bewildered. That scene left a lasting impression on me.

His classic romantic thriller *Charade* starred Audrey Hepburn and Cary Grant. The film is packed with unforgettable moments: George Kennedy menacingly wielding his hook for a hand, James Coburn ending up a corpse with a plastic bag over his head, and Walter Matthau as the creepy villain, aiming his gun at Hepburn in a dark theater before plunging through the trapdoor.

As the last great director from Hollywood's Golden Age, Donen left an indelible mark on the industry. I was lucky to work with two of his talented sons. Josh was instrumental in casting Nia Peeples in my Universal surfing picture, *North Shore*, and Peter was the visual effects supervisor for my Disney film, *Flight of the Navigator*. Both carried on the classy Donen tradition.

When Stanley received his lifetime achievement Oscar in 1997, he charmed the audience with a performance as memorable as his films. "Words seem inadequate," he said. "In musicals, that's when we do a song, so..." Then, he began singing, "Heaven, I'm in Heaven..." When he got to the lyric, "dancing cheek to cheek," he pressed his newly acquired Oscar against his face. He topped it off with a tap dance that got the audience roaring. And he finished up his acceptance with this advice on being a good director: "Show up, get the best people, then get out of the way. But you gotta show up!"

Richard Donner

Richard was one of the most likable and beloved figures in the industry. And if you've enjoyed a superhero movie in the last four decades, you have him to thank. *Superman*, starring Christopher Reeve, set the standard for all comic book films that followed. It had everything—groundbreaking special effects, heartfelt moments, and just the right touch of humor. Richard's genius was in treating the material seriously, rather than satirically or campily. That choice influenced the entire genre.

From the start, he knew *Superman* would only work if the audience truly believed a man could fly. His effects team pulled off an early test using rear projection coupled with a gearhead on the camera. In the demo, Reeve soared forward and banked off to the right. It was so seamless that the crew froze in stunned silence—then burst into cheers. Richard called it "magical and emotional."

Richard also invented the buddy-cop genre with *Lethal Weapon*, pairing Mel Gibson and Danny Glover as two mismatched cops. Their chemistry was electric, leading to three successful sequels. Richard often remarked that Mel Gibson was one of the funniest people he'd ever worked with.

I'll never forget *The Omen*, one of the most chilling films I've ever seen. Richard, however, didn't call it a horror movie when persuading Gregory Peck to take the lead role. Instead, he framed it as a "mystery-suspense thriller." What other director could pull off convincing American icon Peck to attempt to murder a child and stab a woman in the head with an icepick?

One of my favorite stories about Richard comes from screenwriter Brian Helgeland. Brian once took his three-year-old son to the Warner lot, where they ran into Richard. The boy had just seen *Treasure Island* and looked at Richard through plastic binoculars. Richard asked what he was seeing. The kid replied, "Gold." Without missing a beat, Richard shot back, "You're goddamn right!"

I attended a salute to Richard Donner at the Academy's Samuel Goldwyn Theater. His humbleness seemed completely genuine. He talked about starting out directing *Route 66* with my mentor, "the great actress Nina Foch." He admitted that he never really paid his dues, and considered himself "the luckiest guy in Hollywood." At the end of the tribute, his parting words were: "Here's something I never thought I'd say—I'd like to thank the Academy."

Roland Emmerich

Roland Emmerich first came onto my radar when my brother Jeff worked on the visual effects for one of his earliest films, *Stargate*. Since then, Roland has become a master of sci-fi spectacle, crafting films with breathtaking production values and grandiose storytelling. He's often compared to Cecil B. DeMille, though Roland's "casts of thousands" are often digital creations.

Initially aspiring to be a production designer, Roland pivoted to directing after being inspired by George Lucas' *Star Wars*. His production designer roots shine through in films like *The Day After Tomorrow, Godzilla, Independence Day, 10,000 BC, 2012,* and *Moonfall*. Despite their massive scale, his films often incorporate character-driven, emotionally resonant moments. One standout example is the ending of *Moonfall*, where a nerdy character sacrifices himself to save Earth, only to reappear as a consciousness preserved by an AI in the moon's core. The sequence, complete with interactions with avatars of his mother and his cat, is unexpectedly touching—a testament to Roland's ability to balance spectacle with heart.

I was particularly impressed by the sheer scale and visuals of his ancient Rome series, *Those About to Die*. Shot in 108 days, it was his first time working with LED volume stages. He loved the process, especially since it let actors feel immersed in the environment rather than being surrounded by blue screens.

But Roland isn't just about sci-fi and disaster movies. He's ventured into other genres with *The Patriot* and *Midway*, both of which retain his epic visual style. And in 2015, after being rejected by major studios, he financed his passion project, *Stonewall*, a film about the New York riots that sparked the Gay Liberation movement.

Roland is a great host and stages the parties at his home like a movie: a great-looking cast (often peppered with stars from his films), set against the backdrop of his cinematic garden and pool house. I once invited him to a party at my place. He hiked up the canyon in the hot sun only to find he had gotten the date wrong. We had a laugh and a beer.

Federico Fellini

Federico Fellini is my favorite director. Though he initially aspired to be a cartoonist, he channeled that artistic sensibility into developing the distinctive and visually rich style that defines all his films. My personal favorite is *Satyricon*, with its quirky and sensual take on ancient Rome.

Fellini's love affair with cinema began as a child when he saw *Modern Times* by Charlie Chaplin. He was so captivated by its evocative score that he felt compelled to play the theme music on any piano he encountered afterward. Over his career, Fellini earned four Academy Awards for Best Foreign Language Film.

He also introduced the term "paparazzi" to popular culture by naming the relentless photographer in *La Dolce Vita*, "Paparazzo."

Fellini often spoke about cinema with reverence, calling it a "hypnotic, religious ritual." In contrast, he lamented the rise of television that had created a tide of impatient, distracted viewers wielding their remotes, "like a firing squad that deletes faces and words." I wonder what he'd say about social media.

During a publicity tour in Rome for my movie *Summer Lovers*, I wanted to see if there was a way to track him down. It turned out the publicist assigned to my film knew him and made a call. After a few minutes of Italian, she relayed the good news. Fellini was in town, prepping a new movie, had seen and liked *Grease*, and invited me to come to Cinecittà Studios for a visit. I was astounded by my luck. When we reached his office, Fellini greeted me warmly and showed me his hand-drawn storyboards for the film. Then he took me to a soundstage where carpenters were building a massive ocean liner set. After exchanging words with the foreman, he led me on a personal tour of the backlot. He wore his signature black hat and cape and put his arm around my shoulder, pointing out where he had shot scenes from *8 ½*, *La Dolce Vita*, and *Spirits of the Dead*. Some remnants of the old sets were still standing. I wish a photograph could have been taken to document this highlight of my life, but it is vivid in my mind's eye.

Before I left, Fellini presented me with a gift... a large book of conceptual drawings from all his films. He signed it: "To Randal Kleiser, with instant simpatico, Federico Fellini." This is my most prized possession that I keep in a fireproof safe.

Gary Fleder

Gary, a fellow graduate of the USC School of Cinematic Arts, is one of the last of a generation that honed their filmmaking skills by creating Super 8 movies. He recalls the painstaking process of tape splicing and working with magnetic stripes. At USC, Gary directed *Air Time*, a 48-minute short written by his college friend Scott Rosenberg. The film caught the attention of HBO executives, who hired him to direct two episodes of *Tales from the Crypt*.

A few years later, Scott brought Gary, *Things to Do in Denver When You're Dead*, the film that would launch both of their careers. The movie drew comparisons to Quentin Tarantino's work, though its release shortly after *Pulp Fiction* may have overshadowed its impact. Still, it has remained a cult favorite for fans of offbeat, gritty storytelling.

In 1997, Gary and I attended the Deauville Film Festival, where he was debuting his thriller *Kiss the Girls*, starring Ashley Judd and Morgan Freeman. Although The New York Times offered a biting review, calling it "cut from the same cloth as *The Silence of the Lambs*, but…a discarded remnant," the audiences had the final say, and the film became a sleeper hit.

I caught his episode of *Homicide: Life on the Street—The Subway*, featuring Vincent D'Onofrio as a man who gets pinned between a subway train and the platform after being pushed. The character furiously lashes out in pain and anger. The lead detective learns the man will be dead if the train moves and comforts him in his final minutes. Gary broke all the rules about screen direction to heighten the disorientation and suspense. The gripping performance won an Emmy nomination and a Peabody Award.

He later directed *Runaway Jury*, pulling powerful performances from acting legends Gene Hackman and Dustin Hoffman, and cast James Franco against type as a villain in *Homefront*.

I visited Gary on the set of the sci-fi thriller *Impostor* in 2001, where he was commanding a large set featuring a futuristic train. The following year, I invited him to speak at a DGA video conference with students from Miami-Dade College. There, he openly confessed that making *Impostor* was probably a mistake. It was based on a great short story by Philip K. Dick that, in his words, "didn't need expanding." His takeaway? "You can talk yourself into anything for the wrong reasons." The students praised his honesty and openness.

In addition to continuing his directing career, Gary has returned to his alma mater, USC, as adjunct faculty professor.

John Frankenheimer

When we were students at USC, George Lucas and I were driving up the coast and spotted arc lights surrounding a Malibu beach house. We wanted to crash the set, but there were security guards. We later found out it was John Frankenheimer shooting his horror classic *Seconds*—right in his own home. Rock Hudson delivered the best performance of his career in that film, which remains one of my all-time favorites.

I first encountered John a decade later on the Paramount lot. A group of us working on *Grease* walked into a screening room to watch dailies and found John looking at his 16mm home movies of a deep-sea fishing trip. We watched quietly from the back of the room until it was finished. He got up, thanked us, and left.

I wrote him about how much I loved *Seconds*. To my surprise, he sent me a VHS copy of his personal print. (This was before DVDs and streaming, when getting your hands on a movie like that actually meant something.)

Years later, we both appeared on a panel at the DGA. I used the opportunity to tell him how much I admired his political thriller *The Manchurian Candidate*, especially its 360-degree panning sequence where American POWs in Korea are brainwashed during a "garden party." The set and actors shift multiple times throughout a single shot, creating an eerie and disorienting effect. It's said that Frank Sinatra had to get John F. Kennedy's blessing to make the movie, which was chilling since the plot is about a political assassination.

John made so many great movies that warrant repeated viewings, like *Birdman of Alcatraz, Seven Days in May, The Train, Black Sunday*, and *Grand Prix*.

The last time I saw him was in a crowd at the El Capitan Theatre after a screening of his TV movie, *Path to War*. There was a big after-party planned across the street at a Hollywood & Highland nightclub. When I asked John if I could catch up with him there, he shook his head and said he wasn't up for it. Not long after, he passed away.

I will miss this talented artist, whom I consider one of my favorite directors.

Howard Franklin

I've often run into Howard on Sundays at the Farmer's Market on Ivar Avenue in Hollywood. My friend Frederic Golchan produced his film *Quick Change*, a comedy about bungling thieves, starring Bill Murray, Geena Davis, and Randy Quaid. It was Howard's first directing credit, shared with Bill Murray. Because the Directors Guild enforces a strict "one film, one director" rule, they had to face the Western Directors Council to plead their case. The reason? A star could align with a kid right out of film school and push him around. In the case of *Quick Change*, Howard and Bill Murray worked on the script together for months and then went in to make the co-directing request. Howard said it was quite daunting facing all the directors sitting around an oval table with an empty area in the middle, "like a gladiator pit." I get it—as a member of the council, I've sat in on plenty of these requests. At the time, Stanley Kramer was on the council and said, "I'm going to go along with this because you seem like nice boys, but I fear for you in my soul. I fear for one of you when one of you wants to use a 75 mm lens and the other wants to use a 50." Howard and Bill got the waiver, and the comment became a running gag on set. "This is a 75/50 situation!"

Howard next directed Joe Pesci in a terrific performance as a 1940s tabloid photojournalist in *The Public Eye*. Howard had originally hoped to adapt the life of crime photographer Weegee, but when he was unable to secure the rights, he created a fictional story inspired by him. Pesci, too, cited Weegee as a key influence on his character. The film features an offbeat and touching romance between Pesci and Barbara Hershey.

Howard worked with Bill Murray again in the comedy *Larger Than Life*, about a man who inherits an elephant and has to get it across the country in four days to sell it. From personal experience wrangling animals on set, I can confirm it's challenging, but Howard made it look effortless with Murray's huge co-star running, swimming, and knocking things down. Today, it would no doubt be a CGI elephant.

Howard was also one of the writers on *The Name of the Rose*—the medieval mystery adapted from the novel by Umberto Eco and starring Sean Connery and Christian Slater as friars investigating a series of murders in an abbey.

While some directors build recognizable "brands" like Woody Allen and Wes Anderson, Howard prefers to hop between genres, taking a cue from Billy Wilder and Mike Nichols, who refused to be pigeonholed.

Richard Franklin

In the late 1960s, my USC classmate Richard Franklin played a pivotal role in bringing legendary directors onto campus to screen their films and share their wisdom. His most notable achievement was, well before DVDs or VHSs, writing to Alfred Hitchcock to request a screening of *Rope*, which was then out of distribution. To everyone's amazement, Hitchcock himself called Richard to accept the invitation. The real jaw-dropper followed: a three-hour Q&A session that Richard conducted with the Master of Suspense, leaving us all in awe. Richard went on to organize events with John Ford, Orson Welles, and top Disney animators.

Back in his native Sydney, Richard made several low-budget thrillers and became part of the Australian New Wave. According to his contemporary George Miller, back then, Australian directors never sat down on the set. Richard introduced the idea of a director's chair, explaining that he would be emulating the eventual audience who would all be seated.

When *The Blue Lagoon* got the green light, I immediately tapped Richard to produce it with me. Our shooting location was a remote Fijian island with no roads or electricity. We flew in hearty Australian crew members who built a tent city and created a screening area in a grove of palm trees with a generator-powered portable projector. Our "weeklies" were sent by seaplane to Nadi, then by jet to Sydney. When they returned, the crew would sit on blankets in the grove and watch the footage. It was a once-in-a-lifetime experience that would not have happened without Richard.

During *The Blue Lagoon* shoot, Richard was also collaborating with writer Everett De Roche on *Roadgames*. Richard gave him a copy of *Rear Window* for inspiration. After we wrapped, Richard directed the movie, which later earned high praise from Quentin Tarantino for its Hitchcockian flavor. Ultimately, Richard's lifelong passion for Hitchcock came full circle when he directed *Psycho II* for Universal.

Sadly, Richard passed away in 2007 at just 58. His legacy lives on in his films.

Stephen Gaghan

This sketch was done at the Academy when Stephen was promoting *Gold*, his wild drama about a mining scandal. In the first act, Matthew McConaughey's character discovers the world's largest gold mine, and the story then focuses on what happens after achieving your ultimate dream. During the Q&A, Stephen raved about McConaughey's commitment as an artist, highlighting how he transformed himself, shedding his leading-man image to embody an overweight, balding character. The production, set in the jungles of Thailand, faced severe challenges, including a monsoon that nearly shut it down.

Stephen's films are dense and layered. They are best seen more than once to absorb all the information. His projects consistently attract top-tier talent eager to star in a "thinking person's" movie. He won the Oscar for Best Adapted Screenplay for *Traffic*, directed by Steven Soderbergh.

Inspired by the aftermath of 9/11, Stephen tackled the geopolitical thriller *Syriana* as writer-director. The screenplay drew from interviews with oil industry moguls and politicians, and former CIA officer Robert Baer's memoir, *See No Evil*. During his research, Stephen discovered the startling fact that it would only cost one million dollars to overthrow Saddam Hussein. When *Syriana* was screened in Washington, a few politicians stormed out—a reaction Stephen found, let's say, impolite. George Clooney's raw, visceral performance, particularly during the cringeworthy torture scene, left audiences shaken by its realism. Clooney took home the Oscar for Best Supporting Actor.

In a total change of pace, Stephen directed *Dolittle* in 2020, starring Robert Downey Jr. Filmmaking with animals has changed quite a bit since I had Michael Jackson's actual giraffe lick Paul Reubens in *Big Top Pee-wee* back in 1988. For Stephen's version of *Dr. Dolittle*, a CGI giraffe did the fake slobbering on the young lead.

My favorite Stephen Gaghan quote: "The tragedy of Hollywood is all these talented people trying to get excited about stuff they themselves would only view at gunpoint." So true!

Greta Gerwig

When Greta was deciding whether to direct *Barbie*, she knew it could be a career killer if it flopped. There were so many ways it could have gone off the rails.

It didn't.

Greta wound up becoming the first woman director to have a billion-dollar blockbuster, which also makes her the highest-grossing female director of all time. *Barbie* became the highest-grossing movie in Warner Bros. history, with critics just as enthusiastic. I was pleased to learn that *Grease* was one of her influences, and spotting the homages in *Barbie* pretty much made my day.

I first met Greta at a screening of her "semi-autobiographical" directorial debut, *Lady Bird*. In the unforgettable opening scene, Saoirse Ronan's character argues with her on-screen mother, played by Laurie Metcalf, before dramatically leaping out of a moving car. Smash cut to a close-up of her cast, emblazoned with the upside-down message: "Fuck you, Mom." It's a masterclass in locking conflict within the first five minutes. The film is raw and honest, capturing the angst and frustrations of Greta's youth. In one memorable moment, Saoirse's character loses her virginity to Timothée Chalamet's character, only to discover he wasn't a virgin. Disappointed, she says she wanted it to be special, but he shrugs, "Why? You're going to have so much unspecial sex in your life." She fires back, "I was on top! Who is on top their first time?!"

When Greta adapted Louisa May Alcott's *Little Women*, she gave it a modern feminist spin. Greta describes it as "Girl meets boy, girl loses boy, girl gets book...and also the boy."

Greta's journey began in theater, back when she thought movies were almost divine creations, handed down from God. She soon joined an indie group of filmmakers and became part of the "mumblecore" movement, creating films with authenticity and intimacy.

Greta has said that if acting is about listening, then writing is about listening too. When she writes, she tries to listen to what her characters are trying to tell her, discovering who they are. This sounds like a great approach if you can pull it off. And clearly, she does.

Mel Gibson

I did this sketch when Mel was promoting what I consider to be his best film, the moving and uplifting *Hacksaw Ridge*. He told this true story with flawless craftsmanship and excellent performances, especially that of Andrew Garfield. The film received six Oscar nominations. It should have won them all.

I first met Mel in 1980 at a party at his agent Ed Limato's Hollywood Hills home, once owned by Bela Lugosi and still guarded by two bat statues. Mel's striking looks and electric blue eyes hinted at his coming superstardom. We were both early in our careers—he'd just premiered *Mad Max*, and I'd recently directed *The Blue Lagoon*—and it felt like we'd joined an exclusive club.

Mel joked that growing up as one of eleven kids made him feel like "an extra." To stand out, he mastered illusions and practical jokes before eventually enrolling in acting school.

During the *Mad Max* casting, Mel drove a friend to the audition with a bruised face from a recent bar fight. The casting director snapped his photo, thinking, "We need freaks." When Mel returned healed weeks later, George Miller asked him to tell a joke and cast him as the lead on the spot.

After that came *Gallipoli*, *The Bounty*, and the *Lethal Weapon* series, where Mel gave impressive performances. Despite his success, Mel is often self-deprecating. He jokes that Geoffrey Rush told him the fastest way to cry in a scene is to pull a hair out of your nose.

As an actor, he constantly asked questions to understand every part of production. That curiosity served him well when *Braveheart* came along. He only wanted to direct, but financing required him to star as well—so he did. The film went on to win Oscars for Best Picture and Best Director.

Mel wrote, directed, and produced *The Passion of the Christ*, investing its $25 million budget himself. After accusations of antisemitism made traditional distribution impossible, he released the film independently with strong support from church groups. The gamble paid off: it earned over $600 million at the box office.

He went out on a limb again, producing and directing *Apocalypto*. Shot in a Mexican jungle, set in Mayan times, using subtitles and non-actors, the movie was picked up by Disney and shown in 2,500 theaters.

Mel can't be pigeonholed. With *Flight Risk*, he flipped back to action filmmaking.

Terry Gilliam

Terry Gilliam co-directed the funniest comedy scene of all time in *Monty Python's The Meaning of Life*. John Cleese, portraying a French waiter in a posh restaurant, greets his enormous client, Mr. Creosote—played by Terry Jones. Cleese rattles off the menu in a zany French accent as Creosote explosively vomits to the horror of the other diners. My brother Jeff and I have often quoted one of our favorite lines at meals: "And finally, Monsieur... a waffer-theen meent?"

Terry once described Monty Python as "intelligent, silly, surreal, anti-authoritarian—basically six guys who got away with murder." The group was given a surprising free rein by the BBC. Against all odds, their absurdist brand of humor became a global phenomenon. Terry's signature cut-out animations were integral to the Python aesthetic and paved the way for his transition to feature filmmaking.

Initially, he had to adjust to working with real actors instead of paper cutouts, but he adapted quickly. "I love giving actors a chance to do something they haven't done. Brad Pitt was surprisingly and marvelously energetic in *12 Monkeys*."

I spent time with Terry at the 2018 World Immersion Forum in Brussels, where he received a lifetime achievement award and screened his passion project, *The Man Who Killed Don Quixote*—the ultimate example of "development hell." The film spent nearly 30 years in limbo, with a revolving door of lead actors, including Jean Rochefort, John Hurt, and ultimately Jonathan Pryce. Terry and I had a memorable lunch with the "Queen of the Festival," Claudia Cardinale. I had worked with her decades earlier on *Don't Make Waves* with Tony Curtis and Sharon Tate, where I was a surfer extra in her beach scenes. We reflected on how paths randomly cross in the movie business. I loved chatting with Terry about the Python films, his use of wide-angle lenses, and stories behind *Time Bandits* and *Brazil*.

Terry has never been one to hold back his opinions. When a BBC executive claimed that Monty Python wouldn't be greenlit today due to the lack of diversity, Terry quipped, "Well, as a white male, I'm tired of being blamed for everything that is wrong in the world. So from now on, please call me Loretta. I'm a Black lesbian in transition."

When a journalist inquired if he had ever considered retirement, Terry, with his signature quick wit, shot back: "No. Death is more interesting."

Michael Goi

Michael began his career making documentaries and commercials, then racked up over 200 credits as an award-winning cinematographer. He's been president of the American Society of Cinematographers three times, which might explain his massive archive of over 20,000 films. Each week, he shares that passion with a group of up-and-coming students and filmmakers by screening classic films in his home theater.

When I watched his second directed feature, the cult classic *Megan is Missing*, it really affected me. The chilling docudrama follows a teenage girl buried alive by a serial killer. In the final scene, as the killer shovels dirt, you can hear the desperate girl pleading for her life, the sound getting fainter and fainter. Brutal and affecting. This success led to directing assignments for *Pretty Little Liars*, *The Rookie*, *Empire*, and *Riverdale*, among others.

I loved the splashy performance he got from Lady Gaga as a vampire in *American Horror Story*. As a cinematographer, he also developed a memorable visual style for the series: feature film quality on an episodic schedule. Impressive.

Michael shot and directed the thriller *Mary*, starring Gary Oldman, a claustrophobic story set on a haunted boat at sea. He also directed the live-action pilot of *Avatar: The Last Airbender* on one of the largest LED stages in the industry.

On Instagram, he once posted a beautiful video of puffy white clouds floating by a bright blue sky, with the text: "When I fly on a plane, I can't get over the fact that I'm actually FLYING. Others can close their shade and watch TV, but I need to watch views like this." He is a born visual artist.

Michael has always been up to date on the latest technology and joined me as co-chair of the DGA Special Projects Committee that presents our annual Digital Day. The event educates our members on upcoming methods of filmmaking. In turn, Michael asked me to join the board of the Motion Imaging Technology Institute, which he founded and chairs.

Michael Gracey

I first crossed paths with Michael at the famous "Ross House" in the Hollywood Hills, where Academy contenders screen their films for voting members. His film *Better Man* was shown to an appreciative audience.

The bizarre idea of having singer Robbie Williams be portrayed as a monkey was a major challenge for the Weta VFX team. They pulled it off in amazing fashion, capturing every subtle emotion in the ape's face.

I was greatly impressed by the four-minute musical number staged on London's Regent Street. Snappy editing and choreography were planned in a way to dazzle the viewer, and it worked. Originally, the shoot was scheduled the same day Queen Elizabeth II died, which meant everything was canceled—three million dollars down the drain. The studio told Michael to drop it, but he was so determined that he raised the funds himself and returned months later to get the job done. It was worth it.

Michael began his career in his native Australia as a visual effects artist before transitioning to directing music videos and commercials. He made his feature film directorial debut with *The Greatest Showman*. The screenplay, co-written by fellow director Bill Condon, offered a musical interpretation of the life of showman P. T. Barnum, featuring a great performance by Hugh Jackman as the title character. The production values are outstanding: from a scarily realistic fire sequence to a series of high-energy musical numbers. I was particularly taken by the rope-act duet between Zac Efron and Zendaya—beautifully choreographed and edited. Even the CGI elephants look impressively lifelike and integrated into the choreography.

On a personal note, I enjoyed working with one of the film's producers, Laurence Mark, during the production of *Grease*, where he handled publicity.

It was the huge success of *The Greatest Showman* that allowed Michael to go out on a limb with his offbeat approach to *Better Man*. He freely admits that without that hit, his studio pitches would have been cut short, and he would have been shown the door.

Christopher Guest

I am a huge fan of Christopher Guest's comedies, beginning with the groundbreaking *This is Spinal Tap*, directed by his friend Rob Reiner. Christopher played the hilariously clueless rock musician Nigel Tufnel. Rob and Christopher invented the mockumentary genre, with its improvised nature and biting satire. Christopher hates the term. He says it's less about mocking and more about exploring obscure communities.

Right after *Spinal Tap*, he hopped onto *Saturday Night Live*, showing off his knack for off-the-cuff humor. In 1987, Christopher scored another iconic role with Reiner directing: the sadistic six-fingered Count Rugen in *The Princess Bride*.

But making *Spinal Tap* sparked a bigger evolution in his career. He started writing, directing, and acting in his own faux-documentary-style comedies. *Waiting for Guffman*, *Best in Show*, and *A Mighty Wind* stand out from the rest. Using his stock company of actors—Fred Willard, Michael McKean, Jennifer Coolidge, Catherine O'Hara, among many others—Christopher and his writing partner, actor Eugene Levy, mapped out the plot and let actors improvise the dialogue over lengthy takes. This is much more work in the editing room, but the result is comedy genius.

Ricky Gervais once revealed that Christopher was the biggest single influence on his work. He watched *Spinal Tap* over 30 times, and it inspired him to create *The Office*.

Christopher is married to Jamie Lee Curtis, whom I directed in *Grandview USA*. After we wrapped that movie in Pontiac, Illinois, I took my American Airlines AirPass to New York, and Jamie hitched a ride. As I dropped her off, I met Christopher and found this comedic genius to be surprisingly low-key. He comes across as a serious artist.

Jamie explained how she ended up marrying Christopher: she was hanging out with our mutual friend Debra Hill, spotted his photo in a magazine, and announced, "I'm going to marry him." Four months later, she did.

What Jamie never mentioned is that Christopher holds a hereditary British peerage and is officially called Lord Haden-Guest.

I'll be the first in line for any Lord Haden-Guest's projects.

Randa Haines

I caught Randa in this pensive moment after a screening of her film *Dance with Me*. She used to spend four nights a week dancing in Latin clubs, and her love for salsa music led to this project.

Randa discovered Marlee Matlin and cast her in *Children of a Lesser God*. The studio head had a very specific request: "Find me a deaf Debra Winger—sexy, beautiful, and a great actress." Marlee appeared in the background of a casting tape, looking almost childlike, but Randa saw potential and hired her for the lead. To help Marlee embody the mature, sensual character, Randa screened Carlos Saura's *Carmen*. Clearly, that plan worked—Marlee won the Oscar.

Randa's path to filmmaking began in childhood. Thanks to her mother's friendship with Shelley Winters, Randa visited the set of *The Diary of Anne Frank*. She initially considered acting, but eventually found herself drawn to working behind the camera. She took a job as a script supervisor, despite not fully understanding the role. Encouraged by actors with whom she ran lines, she applied to the Directing Workshop for Women at the American Film Institute. This led to directing episodic television, a training ground that honed her ability to think on her feet.

She directed the controversial TV movie *Something About Amelia*. At the time, Ted Danson was starring in the hit series *Cheers* and bravely signed on to play a father who seduces his own daughter. Shortly before the film aired, Randa had a nightmare. She was watching TV and saw a promo for the show, featuring her lead actress in heavy makeup, shouting, "No, Daddy!" Randa awoke screaming, "I didn't shoot that!" When the movie did air, seventeen million people watched it, and the network was swamped by calls from victims of incest.

Years later, the Directors Guild of America invited Randa to Paris to teach a week-long class for emerging French filmmakers. The students' perspectives offered her fresh insights into her own work and rekindled her childhood memories of the city. She began visiting Paris regularly and realized the Los Angeles hustle culture was draining her. Paris, in contrast, invigorated her, offering a renewed perspective on life.

She now calls the City of Lights her base of operations... and living.

Curtis Harrington

Curtis helped launch my career.

During my college days, I met Curtis at a party and told him how much I loved his campy thrillers *Whoever Slew Auntie Roo?* and *What's the Matter with Helen?* I showed him some of my student films, and he offered me my first job in the movie industry as a PA on his next thriller, *The Killing Kind*. My job was bringing coffee to Ann Sothern, John Savage, and Cindy Williams. One unforgettable moment: Ann Sothern kept eating the chocolates being used in a scene. The prop man decided to spray them with Pledge furniture cleaner to stop this. It didn't work. Ms. Sothern devoured them all. My other assignment was picking up extras from an old-age home and bringing them to the set. I was thrilled to be finally working on a 35mm feature film.

Curtis began directing the then-unknown Dennis Hopper in the avant-garde film *Night Tide*. Curtis soon became another of the dozens of directors Roger Corman launched. Roger assigned him to take two Russian sci-fi films, recutting and redubbing them for American audiences. They became *Voyage to the Prehistoric Planet* and *Queen of Blood*.

Curtis was a generous host who often held parties for his industry friends. One evening in 1970, he invited several of us to his Hollywood Hills home for a screening of a 16mm print of the 1945 film *The Picture of Dorian Gray*, starring Hurd Hatfield. The guest of honor? Hatfield himself. As the film played, I couldn't help but steal glances at Hatfield's middle-aged face as he watched his 28-year-old self portray the eternally youthful Dorian. The moment felt like a surreal extension of the story itself.

Curtis' most valuable contribution to my career was a timely piece of advice. For my USC master's thesis, I had adapted a local theater group's play, but midway through production, I ran out of funding. After reviewing the footage, Curtis urged me to scrap it and do something personal, like the short films I'd shown him. I heeded his advice and made *Peege*, a story about my family's Christmas visit to my grandmother in a nursing home. Upon its completion, I secured a directing contract at Universal.

Curtis passed away in 2007, and I remain eternally grateful for his guidance.

CURTIS HARRINGTON

Anthony Harvey

In my senior year at USC, I met Anthony Harvey, who directed *The Lion in Winter* and edited Stanley Kubrick's *Dr. Strangelove*. Director James Bridges introduced us, and I managed to get Tony to watch my 16mm senior film projected onto my Santa Monica apartment door. He offered encouraging feedback, and a friendship developed.

I remember him struggling over offers to direct *Love Story* and *Cabaret*—both of which he ultimately turned down and later regretted. He did, however, direct *The Abdication*, starring Liv Ullmann and Peter Finch. I'd hoped to work as his assistant on that film in England, but it wasn't in the cards.

Years later, I was watching the film adaptation of George Bernard Shaw's *Caesar and Cleopatra*, starring Vivien Leigh, when the teenage actor playing Cleopatra's younger brother, Ptolemy, looked oddly familiar. When I looked it up on IMDb, I was surprised to find it was Tony's one acting gig. After studying at the Royal Academy of Dramatic Art, he realized he preferred editing.

He then edited *The L-Shaped Room* for Bryan Forbes, then *Lolita* for Stanley Kubrick. While working on *Dr. Strangelove*, Kubrick told him, in essence, "If you're going to be this annoying in the editing room, you should direct!" Tony followed Kubrick's advice and directed the 55-minute film *Dutchman*. Peter O'Toole saw it and lobbied for him to direct *The Lion in Winter*. After meeting Katharine Hepburn, the deal was sealed. The film was nominated for seven Oscars, and Hepburn won Best Actress, sharing it with Barbra Streisand.

The film sparked his lifelong friendship with Katharine Hepburn and several more projects. I always hoped we'd have dinner with her since he constantly spoke of "Kate." That didn't happen.

Tony passed away in 2017 at age 87.

Todd Haynes

Todd first turned heads with his offbeat short *Superstar: The Karen Carpenter Story*. He cast Barbie dolls to act out Karen's rise to stardom and her tragic death from anorexia. Karen's brother sued Todd to stop distributing the film. At my request, Todd kindly sent me a VHS of this no-longer-available cult classic, which I have since lost. (I hear bootlegs might still float around online if you know where to look.)

Todd's films have often explored non-conforming relationships—interracial, lesbian, or age-gap romances. In *Far from Heaven*, Julianne Moore plays a '50s wife who falls in love with her African-American gardener, while Dennis Quaid plays her closeted husband. Todd wanted to make a film without a villain and focus on people wrestling with their desires. I moderated a DGA Q&A with him, where he mentioned being inspired by the style of the films of Max Ophüls and Douglas Sirk. He also told a great story about composer Elmer Bernstein insisting on no temp music—until he discovered Todd had temped the cut with Bernstein's previous scores. I also loved *Carol*, another gay-themed feature set in the '50s, where Cate Blanchett and Rooney Mara give moving performances as furtive lovers in New York.

Todd reinvented the music biopic with *Velvet Goldmine*, taking a cue from 1970s glam rock, and pushed it even further in *I'm Not There*, his dreamlike take on Bob Dylan, where Christian Bale, Richard Gere, Heath Ledger, and even Cate Blanchett play different aspects of Bob Dylan's personality.

During pre-production for *Safe*, Todd called me to discuss suppressed immune systems since I had tackled that topic in *The Boy in the Plastic Bubble*, about a young boy with no protection against germs. In his film, Julianne Moore portrayed a character with a similar affliction.

Later, Todd turned to documentaries with the very entertaining *The Velvet Underground*, which used a multiscreen format and merged vintage footage with interviews of the famous rock band's members.

Todd continued his exploration of unconventional relationships with *May December*, which follows an actress studying the real-life woman she's about to portray—someone who had an affair with and married an underage student. Once again, Todd dove into edgy territory and emerged with a distinctly human story.

Matthew Heineman

Matthew Heineman is renowned for his award-winning documentaries, each one offering an up-close, deeply personal look at his subjects. In *Cartel Land*, executive produced by Kathryn Bigelow, Matthew embedded himself with vigilante groups confronting Mexican drug cartels. It took months to earn their trust, and at one point, he infiltrated a meth lab. The shoot was terrifying because he often couldn't tell who the good guys were. I was amazed to see real footage of a shootout between vigilantes and the cartel, torture scenes, and severed heads lying on the ground. One striking moment showed a grandmother physically pushing back a cop car. He exposed corruption and betrayals on all sides. The film earned an Oscar nomination for Best Documentary Feature and won three Primetime Emmys.

City of Ghosts came next, chronicling a group of Syrian media activists challenging ISIS' takeover of their country, constantly on the run and documenting their undercover work. Again, his camera was in the middle of shootouts. As Matthew puts it, "My goal always is to make you feel like you're there and think, 'What would I do?'"

In 2018, he turned to narrative filmmaking with the thrillingly realistic *A Private War*. Rosamund Pike delivers a gripping performance as war reporter Marie Colvin. His documentary instincts are extremely evident in the film's raw, realistic style, which critics praised.

Matthew followed up with *The Trade*, a series examining the opioid crisis in a way reminiscent of Steven Soderbergh's *Traffic*. He also captured Colombian reggaeton singer J. Balvin facing political controversy in *The Boy from Medellin*, and then turned the camera on golf icon Tiger Woods in *Tiger*.

Matthew claims that the hardest film he has ever made is his gut-wrenching COVID documentary, *The First Wave*. Shot in New York City at the pandemic's height, he risked his life to follow the nurses and doctors 24/7 as they dealt with the deadly disease. He compared the experience to filming in a war zone. It's tough to watch but very moving.

When Matthew directed *American Symphony*, he originally intended to follow the creative process of Jon Batiste composing his first symphony. The documentary took an emotional turn when Batiste's wife, Suleika, was diagnosed with cancer. Matthew pivoted the focus, and the film gained a whole new layer of depth. As one of his mentors once told him, "If you end up with the story you started with, you weren't listening along the way." And clearly, Matthew is a good listener.

Werner Herzog

I crossed paths with Werner Herzog in 2015 at the annual Directors Breakfast hosted by Robert Redford during the Sundance Film Festival. Werner sat at a table surrounded by young filmmakers. Engaged in lively conversation, he connected with the group as if he were one of their peers. Most of them recognized him for his legendary films like *Aguirre, the Wrath of God*, *Fitzcarraldo*, and *Wings of Hope*.

As a young man, Werner Herzog shared an apartment with the famously eccentric actor Klaus Kinski, whom he later directed in five films. Reflecting on their tumultuous relationship, Herzog once joked, "Every gray hair on my head I call Kinski." His particular sense of humor has taken its toll on him a few times. Once, he jumped on a cactus after completing the troubled filming of *Even Dwarfs Started Small*. Years later, he famously promised to eat his shoe if filmmaker Errol Morris could ever complete his first movie. When the film materialized, Werner kept his word. Les Blank immortalized the event in the documentary *Werner Herzog Eats His Shoe*.

His film *Fitzcarraldo* tells the story of a dreamer who attempts to haul a huge boat over a mountain in the Amazon jungle. The making of this movie was such a Herculean task—complete with hostile natives, disease, and the savagery of nature—that it spawned its own documentary, *Burden of Dreams*, capturing Werner's ability to tackle the impossible.

Despite directing, writing, and producing over sixty acclaimed features and documentaries, he might be best known to the younger generations as The Client in the *Star Wars* series *The Mandalorian*. Fans of the show also owe him the fact that no CGI was used with Grogu (Baby Yoda). When the creators tried to replace the puppet in a scene, Werner snapped at them, "You're cowards, leave it!"

Before all this, Werner worked as a welder in Germany, a night fisherman in Greece, and—without knowing how to ride a horse—served as a rodeo clown in Mexico. In the age of technology, Werner remains a self-styled globetrotter who travels light and on foot. He doesn't even own a cellphone. Werner insists that if he knocks on a stranger's door, they'll likely invite him for a meal: "The world reveals itself to those who travel by foot." A fitting mantra for someone who prefers true human contact.

"A director has to be self-reliant, bold, and has to seize the occasion and move in the *mud*."

Tom Hooper

I loved *The King's Speech*. In his Best Director Oscar acceptance speech, Tom thanked his Australian mum for a tip she gave him after attending a fringe theater reading of the play in London. She called him and said, "Tom, I think I've found your next film." He concluded his speech by saying, "So with this tonight, I honor you, and the moral is: listen to your mother."

As a teen, Tom made short films and later directed plays at Oxford University. He then moved into directing British TV episodes before breaking into feature films with *Red Dust*.

After his success with *The King's Speech*, I was curious to see how Tom would do the movie adaptation of the musical *Les Misérables*. At a screening at the Academy's Samuel Goldwyn Theater, where most of the cast was present, I was inspired by the production, particularly the number "One Day More," which combined many of the film's major themes. After the Q&A, I was able to catch up with Helena Bonham Carter, whom I had worked with on my film *Getting It Right*. I loved her performance, and we chatted about the fact that all the singing was performed live with lavalier mics taped to the costumes, and then digitally removed. I later watched the Blu-ray several times, looking for signs of the digital cleanup with no luck.

In directing *The Danish Girl*, about one of the first recipients of gender-affirming surgery, Tom noted that, "If you are a woman and your male self is a mask, then playing a man would feel like a suit of armor he was putting on to suppress his femininity."

Knowing how much effort went into *Cats*, I was sad to see it misfire. It was clear that teams of visual effects artists had gone over every frame, adding fur and tails to dozens of actors. I thought it was unfair for this team to be the brunt of a joke at that year's Academy Awards. However, the one thing about *Cats* that no one seemed to mention was the fantastic production design. The sets that Tom and his artists created were stunning.

In working with performers, Tom commented, "The really great actors have a kind of mise-en-scène in their head and arrive on set with ways to stage it, and have a director's mind as well as an actor's, and I always try to respect that."

Reginald Hudlin

Reginald Hudlin has had a varied career: President and Head of Programming for Black Entertainment Television, producer of the Oscars, writer of the graphic novel *Black Panther*, executive producer of the NAACP Image Awards, and producer of Tarantino's *Django Unchained*.

Reginald's paternal great-great-grandfather was Peter Hudlin, who was involved in the *Underground Railroad*.

He started out at Harvard, making the comedy short *House Party*, which he later expanded into the hit feature. The success of his film debut led him to direct Eddie Murphy, Halle Berry, Chris Rock, David Alan Grier, and Martin Lawrence in the cult comedy, *Boomerang*.

I met Reginald at the mixing session for *Marshall*, which my good friend Jonathan Sanger produced. Chadwick Boseman took the role of Thurgood Marshall, the first African-American Supreme Court Justice. Reginald got great performances and excellent chemistry from Boseman, Kate Hudson, and James Cromwell. I enjoyed seeing the final film and liked Diane Warren's and Common's stirring end title anthem "Stand Up For Something."

Reginald directed many episodic shows and produced *The Black Godfather* about Clarence Avant. The doc has appearances by Quincy Jones, Bill Clinton, Snoop Dog, David Geffen, and Barack Obama, all talking about this behind-the-scenes genius.

Reginald directed *The Kamala Harris Story* during the 2024 election. Unfortunately, even with Morgan Freeman involved, Kamala did not prevail.

His advice to aspiring filmmakers? "You have a supercomputer in your pocket. You can study international films, read scripts, shoot a movie, edit a movie, and distribute it all over the world. Use what's around you and do the most with what you have."

John Huston

John Huston replaced me as director of the movie *Annie*.

After making *The Blue Lagoon*, I was hired to direct the movie by David Begelman. When Ray Stark took over as producer, there was a lack of chemistry between us. I wanted to experiment with computer graphics sets, and Ray didn't get it. He wanted to work with his old pal, John Huston, and fired me.

I have enjoyed John Huston's many classic films: *The Maltese Falcon*, *The Treasure of the Sierra Madre*, *The Asphalt Jungle*, *The African Queen*, *The Man Who Would Be King*, and *Prizzi's Honor*.

Behind the scenes, Huston was just as fascinating. While filming *The Misfits*, he admitted Marilyn Monroe's constant back-and-forth with her acting coach drove him up the wall.

His film *Beat the Devil* confused the studio and audiences when it was first released—nobody realized it was a dark comedy until years later, and it has since become a cult classic. During the shooting, Huston recalled a surreal moment when Humphrey Bogart and Truman Capote got into a wrestling match, and to everyone's surprise, Capote pinned Bogie to the floor.

Though Huston usually wrote his own films, he hired Ray Bradbury for *Moby Dick*. Their creative clash inspired Bradbury to pen a short story called *Banshee*.

During his long career, Huston also acted. He played a Boston cardinal in Otto Preminger's *The Cardinal*, earning him an Academy Award nomination for Best Supporting Actor. He appeared in *Chinatown* for Roman Polanski and in *The Wind and the Lion* for my USC classmate John Milius. He even played a character based on Orson Welles in Welles' last completed film, *The Other Side of the Wind*, and had a part in *Myra Breckinridge*, though he apparently avoided seeing it.

Regarding *Annie*, it was the first of two times I was fired from a movie. Not fun, but at least I can say I was replaced with John Huston.

Peter Hyams

Peter is known as a combination of cinematographer and director. He has held both positions on over a dozen features. Having studied art and becoming a celebrated painter, his films reflect great attention to composition and lighting. I have admired his varied career from the memorable train action sequence in *Narrow Margin* to the visual effects of his many sci-fi movies.

As a fan of the sci-fi genre, I enjoyed the Space Western, *Outland*, with Sean Connery, *Capricorn One* with its premise of a fake Mars landing, *Timecop* with Van Damme, *End of Days* with Schwarzenegger fighting the devil, and the sequel to Kubrick's *2001*, *2010: The Year We Make Contact*.

In 2005, he brought his feature *A Sound of Thunder* to our annual Digital Day at the DGA. It was based on a book by Ray Bradbury, whom I met when I was a student at USC. It was a thrill to ask Ray to join Peter for the screening. Afterward, Ray took center stage with a folder on his lap, delivered an inspiring 40-minute talk without looking at his notes, and got a standing ovation. I later asked Ray to see his folder and found that they were blank pages.

Peter is not a fan of the handheld camera. "Camera shaking and zooming half in and half out is not reality. We actually have a steadicam in our head. When we run, the world doesn't shake; otherwise, everyone would throw up."

Some of his favorite filmmakers are Ridley Scott, Steven Spielberg, and Alfonso Cuarón, "Directors who tell the story rather than calling attention to themselves."

Peter has handled action, dramas, comedies, and thrillers. I agree with him when he says, "Everyone in the industry is either overrated or underrated."

Mick Jackson

Mick directed the best satire of Hollywood, *L.A. Story*, starring Steve Martin. The laugh-out-loud moments captured the craziness of the town. Mick initially thought that, being English, he might not be right for the project, but Steve Martin wanted an outsider's look at Tinseltown. He drove Mick around LA, showing him some of the nuttier sights. Mick accepted the assignment and used his European sensibility to create a fresh take. "The light in LA, particularly at night through the palm trees, is like an impressionist painting." He wanted to show people doing silly things, but not caring, and added French music with a calm quality. Charles Trenet's "La Mer" is not the kind of music one would think of for Los Angeles.

Another comedy he directed was *Clean Slate*, with Dana Carvey, about a murder witness with amnesia.

Switching genres, he directed the popular romantic thriller, *The Bodyguard*, starring Kevin Costner and Whitney Houston. The film featured Houston's hit cover of Dolly Parton's "I Will Always Love You," the best-selling movie soundtrack of all time, with 45 million copies.

A film he directed about nuclear war called *Threads* for the BBC got terrific reviews and has been called "the most terrifying movie of all time" and "guaranteed to give you nightmares." This led to him creating, quite realistically, lava erupting from the La Brea Tar Pits in *Volcano*. And this was before CGI.

Could the same director have done a movie about Holocaust deniers? Yes. It was titled *Denial* and starred Rachel Weisz.

With *Temple Grandin*, Mick explored the lead character's autism and won an Emmy Award for Outstanding Directing. Claire Danes won Best Actress.

It's always interesting to see where Mick will take us next.

Peter Jackson

I was extremely impressed by Peter Jackson's *The Lord of the Rings* and *The Hobbit* trilogies with their stunning production design and groundbreaking visual effects. He created the first CGI character that felt like a living being, the surreal Gollum. He was also the first director to use Massive software, which can digitally simulate thousands of realistic extras swarming across the screen. Making the film was extremely challenging. Early on, *The Lord of the Rings* nearly lost its financing, and Peter was at risk of losing his house, which he had borrowed money against. Luckily, things worked out.

Always pushing boundaries, Peter combined the traditional technique of forced perspective with the cutting-edge SimulCam technology to create moving camera shots of Ian McKellen's Gandalf surrounded by dwarves in *The Hobbit: An Unexpected Journey*. He was one of the first directors to experiment with high frame rate to give a more realistic look to the images, although some said it was too sharp and felt like live HDTV.

As a kid, he built dinosaur figures and was a big fan of the *Batman* and *Thunderbirds* TV series. He got a Super 8mm camera and started shooting his dinosaurs. He even played James Bond in an early short where he learned to edit. But the real game-changer was *King Kong*, the movie that made him want to be a filmmaker. You can see his affection for Kong in his 2005 remake that brought 1930s New York City stylishly to life and gave an amazing look to Skull Island.

In his documentary film, *They Shall Not Grow Old*, he turned his digital skills to restoring film footage from World War I in a startling way. He colorized the material, changed the speed to make the movements more lifelike, hired lip readers to analyze what the soldiers were saying, and directed actors to perform the words.

His restoration expertise was next used to create *The Beatles: Get Back*, a "documentary about a documentary" lasting nearly eight hours and revealing an intimate side to the group not seen before. The project was made by going through 57 hours of footage shot during the recording session for their album "Let It Be." Peter observed that Paul was saddened to see Yoko Ono slowly becoming the voice that John listened to, rather than himself.

I love cutting-edge technology and how it can be adapted to storytelling. Peter hooked up with Steven Spielberg to use CGI and motion capture to bring the books of *Tintin* to life. Both men are true visionaries of the future of cinema.

Jim Jarmusch

In 1984, I saw Jim's debut feature, *Stranger Than Paradise*, and was struck by its unusual style. Shot in black in white—using short ends gifted by Wim Wenders—it unfolds in a series of master shots, each separated by a black screen. At the time, I didn't fully understand the technique, but later learned that Jim wanted the last image of each scene to linger. Clearly, it worked—the film was added to the National Registry in 2002.

Jim was influenced by experimental filmmaker Jonas Mekas, who cared more about art than money. He was infected by Mekas' enthusiasm for learning new things, "I consider myself a dilettante—there are too many things in the world to just focus on one or two of them. I take in things from many sources and forms." Another key influence was Nicholas Ray, Jim's teacher at NYU, whom he worked for as an assistant.

Offbeat is how I would describe most of his films. Jim is one of the pioneers of the American indie movement and loves exploring the "fish out of water" theme. *Down by Law* follows three mismatched convicts escaping from a New Orleans jail. *Mystery Train* tells three interconnected, separate stories with eclectic characters in a Memphis flophouse. *Dead Man* is a psychedelic Western with Johnny Depp, Iggy Pop, and Robert Mitchum. *Paterson* observes a week in the life of Paterson, a bus driver-poet in the town of Paterson, New Jersey. *Broken Flowers* follows Bill Murray as a man searching for a son he didn't know he had. And then there's *Ghost Dog: The Way of the Samurai*—possibly his toughest film—where Forest Whitaker plays a contract killer who lives by the samurai code.

He transitioned to mainstream Hollywood with *The Dead Don't Die*, featuring his most commercial cast: Adam Driver, Tilda Swinton, Tom Waits, Selena Gomez, and Bill Murray. A comedy about zombies; it harkened back to the monster movies Jim loved as a kid, *Attack of the Crab Monsters* and *Creature from the Black Lagoon*. Dark and satirical, the movie has several laugh-out-loud moments. He then cast Waits as Driver's father in *Father Mother Sister Brother*, which also featured two of my favorites; Charlotte Rampling and Cate Blanchett.

"Don't look for the obvious, always keep your eyes open, keep thinking on your feet, and be open."

Rian Johnson

When Rian was a film student at USC, I hosted a cast and crew party at my home for his short, *Evil Demon Golfball from Hell!!!* Even then, it was clear he was going places.

His first feature, *Brick*, was a labor of love that took a decade to bring to life. With financial help from his grandfather, Rian wrote and directed the mystery on a shoestring budget of less than half a million dollars. When *Brick* premiered at Sundance, the audience was enthusiastic, but for Rian, the highlight was seeing his family behind him, beaming with pride. The film grossed nearly $4 million, and he was thrilled to pay his grandfather back.

Working with the constraints of episodic television, Rian still brought a cinematic flair to his *Breaking Bad* episode, *Fly*.

Next, he tackled sci-fi with *Looper*, a sleek time-travel thriller inspired by *The Terminator*. His goal was to create a tight, conceptually sound film, and it paid off with good reviews and box office success. That led to him writing and directing *Star Wars: The Last Jedi*, which grossed over $1 billion.

A devoted Agatha Christie fan, Rian then turned to the comedy-mystery genre with *Knives Out*, a film packed with twists and a stellar cast, including Daniel Craig, Chris Evans, and my friend Jamie Lee Curtis. Jamie, by the way, is a national treasure. Back when we were filming *Grandview USA*, she brought pizzas for the cast and crew on a night shoot, even though she wasn't even on the call sheet.

In *Knives Out*, Rian explored how families deal with opposite political views. The film earned him an Oscar nomination for Best Original Screenplay and was such a hit that he landed a deal for two sequels. He kept Daniel Craig as the central character, describing him as having "the gravity of a thousand suns in terms of charisma." His *Wake Up Dead Man* is his most personal film in the franchise and deals with how beliefs and faith intersect with society.

Plot twists are a signature of Rian's work. He likens them to a magician doing a card trick—they work best when the audience is distracted by misdirection. This is on full display in his series for Peacock, *Poker Face*.

His website features several short films, including a poignant music video starring Sissy Spacek and David Strathairn. I found the ending moving and highly recommend giving it a watch.

Spike Jonze

Spike Jonze is a modern-day renaissance man. He is an accomplished musician, photographer, actor, and director of documentaries, commercials, music videos, and feature films.

He began his career as a teenage photographer, capturing skateboarders for magazines and earning him credibility within the community. Building on this momentum, he launched his own magazine dedicated to the sport. Along the way, he honed his skills in composition and technique by learning from other photographers. These experiences culminated in his first short film, *Video Days*, a project centered on skateboarding.

His distinctive style caught the attention of the music industry, leading to music video collaborations with iconic artists like Daft Punk, Björk, and Sonic Youth. He later co-created MTV's *Jackass* alongside Johnny Knoxville, a reality franchise infamous for its wild and often painful stunts. While the cast specialized in pranking each other, Spike wasn't off-limits—once, he rang a doorbell only to get smacked in the face by a triggered airbag. The show's chaotic energy peaked in its fourth episode when Knoxville was hospitalized after a bull sent him flying.

For his first feature, *Being John Malkovich*, Spike received a Best Director Oscar nomination. He credits Malkovich for launching his career and thanks him every time he sees him. I saw some behind-the-scenes footage of Spike shooting on the set of the 7 ½ floor. The actors and crew complained of sprained necks and kept banging their heads on the low ceilings.

Spike later won an Oscar for Best Screenplay with *Her*, inspired by an early AI chat program that made him wonder if a person could eventually develop a real relationship with an artificial intelligence. At the time, the idea seemed futuristic, but now AI companions are a reality.

Beyond directing, Spike has taken on acting roles, playing the lead character in David O. Russell's war comedy *Three Kings* and a supporting role in Martin Scorsese's *The Wolf of Wall Street*.

After the attacks on the World Trade Center in 2001, the CIA reached out to USC's Institute for Creative Technologies to form a think tank of filmmakers tasked with imagining possible future terrorist scenarios. I was teamed with Spike Jonze and David Fincher. I could reveal more, but then I'd have to kill you.

Jonathan Kaplan

Jonathan is best known for his hit film *The Accused*. I recently rewatched it and was struck by how effectively he puts the viewer in Jodie Foster's character's shoes. The structure of the movie is interesting. It begins with Jodie running from a bar where she was raped, and follows her to the hospital, then through all the attempts to get help, meeting a lawyer, and describing what happened. It is not until the trial that the assault is shown in horrific detail. Jodie Foster won the Oscar for her performance.

Jonathan grew up surrounded by show business. His father was a composer, his mother an actress. He started as a child actor on Broadway in *The Dark at the Top of the Stairs*, directed by Elia Kazan. In films, he worked under Arthur Hiller in *Plaza Suite* and Martin Ritt in *The Molly Maguires*.

At NYU, he studied under Martin Scorsese and won the grand prize for a student film. Impressed by his work, Scorsese recommended him to Roger Corman, who gave him his first feature assignment, *Night Call Nurses*. He later directed *Heart Like a Wheel*, about drag racer Shirley Muldowney, and the sci-fi drama *Project X*, starring Helen Hunt, Matthew Broderick, and a chimpanzee. Michelle Pfeiffer worked with Jonathan on *Love Field* and received a Best Actress nomination.

Along the way, he directed two "blaxploitation" films, *The Slams* starring former football player Jim Brown, and *Truck Turner*, with soul artist Isaac Hayes.

His biggest failure was *Mr. Billion*, which he explained in an amusing YouTube video. He was 29 and had just finished directing the successful *White Line Fever*. Dino De Laurentiis wanted a movie that would introduce Terence Hill to the English-speaking world. His first day of shooting in Italy was daunting—he had to direct Jackie Gleason, who was grumpy because none of the Italians knew who he was. Jackie pulled Jonathan aside, nodded to Hill, and said, "The kid is a lox, the picture's a bomb, but I'm gonna give you everything I've got." Jackie, however, would drink six bottles of Dom Perignon a day. Jonathan figured out that if he quoted *Honeymooner* routines, the Americans on the crew would laugh and Jackie would sober up long enough to get through his scenes. A clever workaround. The picture bombed, but he got to work with Gleason.

Jonathan has been very successful in television with the series *ER*, for which he got five Emmy nominations for producing and directing.

Joanna Kerns

Joanna started out as an actress, studying with renowned acting teacher Peggy Feury. Others in the class were Michelle Pfeiffer, Tom Cruise, Sean Penn, and Jeff Goldblum. After working as a chorus girl for Gene Kelly and a gold digger for Dean Martin, Joanna began appearing in dozens of movies and TV shows, and eventually became best known for her eight-year run on the TV series *Growing Pains*.

After managing to get a directing assignment on the show, she had a hard time getting her next directing job. At the time, women directors were practically unheard of. One executive bluntly told her, "We tried a woman, and it didn't work out." But Joanna didn't give up—she kept pushing and was finally able to get a foothold. As one of the first female television directors, she paved the way for others. She has over 70 (yes, 70!) directing credits on shows like *Dawson's Creek*, *ER*, *Pretty Little Liars*, *Grey's Anatomy*, *The Good Doctor*, *This is Us*, and *Chicago Med*.

Joanna became a producer on *A Million Little Things* and was proud of the fact that half of the directors were women. She also juggled the series through the COVID pandemic, where she had to close the production down several times.

Joanna explains that shooting a four-camera sitcom, the format popularized by Lucille Ball and Desi Arnaz, is like putting on a play. When directing a single-camera dramatic film, she's developed her own method, using three cameras for every setup. As she puts it, "Directing is infinitely complex, scary, and exciting."

Little-known fact: Joanna nearly made the 1968 Olympics team as a gymnast. Her sister Donna won two gold Olympic medals in swimming and appeared on the cover of Sports Illustrated. Joanna later wrote a screenplay based on her family that she jokingly refers to as *I Never Swam for My Father*.

Joanna co-founded the Lucy Awards, which honored both men and women whose work enhanced the perception of women in television. She is very active at the DGA—we served together on the Western Directors Council and the National Board. She continues to give back through the Directors Guild Foundation, which supports members in financial hardship and teaches professional standards to up-and-coming directors in the DGA's New Directors workshop.

Regina King

I was seated behind Regina when I did this sketch.

She won the Best Supporting Actress Oscar for her role in Barry Jenkins' feature *If Beale Street Could Talk*. Throughout her career, Regina has learned from great directors like Jenkins, who taught her how important attention to detail can be, especially for crafting memorable moments that aren't always spelled out in the screenplay. She credits Paris Barclay with boosting her confidence after he praised the visual style of a music video she directed. Regina also picked up essential directing tools from my friend John Singleton, with whom she worked on *Poetic Justice* and *Boyz n the Hood*. John openly shared his methods and creative process, especially the power of storyboards.

Her directing career began on shows like *Scandal* and *This Is Us*. Her first feature was the award-winning *One Night in Miami...* The movie imagines an encounter between Malcolm X, Jim Brown, Sam Cooke, and Muhammad Ali—taking place, as you might guess, one night in Miami. Since the film was adapted from a play, Regina knew she had to keep the camera moving, but not distracting. Because of her acting background, she instinctively knew each actor required a personalized approach, and with only one day of rehearsal, Regina jumped right in. The film was nominated for three Academy Awards.

Regina directed three episodes of the Netflix miniseries *Man in Full*, about a nasty real estate mogul played by Jeff Daniels going through bankruptcy. In the last episode, she created a unique blend of eroticism, violence, and humor, unlike anything I've ever seen before.

Then, she jumped back into acting and producing with her film *Shirley*, a biopic of the first black congresswoman Shirley Chisholm.

Regina calls herself a "controlled enthusiast." In 2019, *Time* magazine named her one of the 100 most influential people in the world. When asked what the best piece of advice she's ever been given, Regina quoted her mother, "The seven P's...proper prior preparation prevents piss poor performance." But I especially like her technique for handling stress: she keeps a jump rope handy, and when things get tense, she will jump for two minutes.

I hope that one day I'll have the opportunity to sketch her from the front.

Stanley Kramer

I felt like a fan when I met Stanley Kramer at a book signing of his autobiography, *A Mad, Mad, Mad, Mad World: A Life in Hollywood*. Here was the man whose groundbreaking films had taught me so much when I was growing up in suburban Philadelphia. The fear of nuclear destruction was on my mind, and he dramatized it brilliantly with *On the Beach*. My first exposure to the Holocaust was through *Judgment at Nuremberg*. In *The Defiant Ones*, he told the story of two escaped convicts, one black and one white, who were shackled together and had to get along. That was my intro to racial conflicts, which he continued with *Guess Who's Coming to Dinner*.

His many films racked up 16 Academy Awards and 80 nominations. Actors respected him because he was honest, sometimes brutally so. Katharine Hepburn once made the mistake of asking a writer to change the name of a character. Stanley called her up and told her to keep her "trap" shut and never give writers suggestions—Katharine loved it.

In 1955, Stanley bravely went on the BBC to talk about his flops. He felt that critics had been too harsh with his film *Not as a Stranger*, driving audiences away from a film he was sure they'd enjoy. Another thorn in his side was the censor, who forced him to cut out a shot of a beating heart in an open chest. He thought it added a dramatic realism that the viewer needed to be exposed to for the sake of the storytelling. When someone asked him why *Cyrano de Bergerac* didn't do well, Stanley humbly replied, "I didn't make it well enough." And when asked about his biggest compromise, he cited *The Caine Mutiny*, a film about naval officers who faced severe consequences after questioning their captain's paranoid orders. It was the only film he ever made that promoted a message he didn't believe in.

In November of 2013, I was honored to receive the first annual Stanley Kramer Lifetime Achievement Award from his widow, Karen, and daughter Kat at the Camelot Theater in Palm Springs, as part of the Stanley Kramer Film Festival.

I'm glad I met him in person. Stanley Kramer is a director whose films I will continue watching over and over.

John Landis

In 2021, I went to John's house to get him to sign my copy of his excellent book, *Monsters in the Movies*. The book featured many of the images we'd both loved in our formative years: Boris Karloff as *The Mummy*, Bela Lugosi as *Dracula*, and Lon Chaney Jr. as *The Wolf Man*, among others. Like John, I was a childhood fan of *Famous Monsters of Filmland*. This monthly magazine wasn't just cool because of the creepy creatures; it was our only window into the world of behind-the-scenes filmmaking. Back then, we had no *Entertainment Tonight*, no DVD commentaries, no YouTube, and no podcasts. We had only *Famous Monsters*—and it was everything.

I'm an admirer of John's films, *National Lampoon's Animal House*, *The Blues Brothers*, *An American Werewolf in London*, *Trading Places*, and Michael Jackson's music video *Thriller*. His wife, Deborah Nadoolman, has designed costumes for many of his films—my favorite being the spectacular African outfits in *Coming to America*.

John once mentioned that he and Joe Dante are the only DGA members who've never taken a possessory credit—they feel filmmaking is a team effort.

On the Universal lot, John befriended Alfred Hitchcock, sharing lunches with him every other week for three years. At one point, John explained to Hitchcock that Brian De Palma was not stealing from him with *Obsession*, but doing an homage. Hitchcock dryly replied, "You mean fromage?"

For fun, John operated the Grover puppet in the final musical number of *The Muppet Movie*. Controlling another puppet was a young, unknown Tim Burton, who was starstruck at meeting the director of *Animal House*.

John and I were the first movie directors to join the Visual Effects Society. In 2005, we proudly presented an award together at their annual ceremony.

There's a troubling trend in Hollywood these days: studios reimagining past hit movies without input from the original directors. It happened to John with *Coming to America*, Paul Schrader with *American Gigolo*, and to me with *The Blue Lagoon* and *Grease*.

John's advice for up-and-coming filmmakers is straightforward: "Write scripts and make movies with your iPhone."

Yorgos Lanthimos

I did this sketch after a screening of Yorgos Lanthimos' mind-blowing *Poor Things* at the Directors Guild. Most of the film's sets were full-size, hand-built using real materials, with digital extensions added when necessary. One particularly memorable sequence, set on a dreamlike vessel, used a giant LED screen as its background. I was impressed by Yorgos' good taste and skill in combining technology with craftsmanship.

Yorgos grew up in Greece at a time when becoming a filmmaker was considered obscure and impractical. Nevertheless, he entered the Stavrakos Film School and started his career shooting dance videos. From there, he moved into commercials and music videos. His distinctively dark humor first gained widespread attention with *The Lobster*, a film about guests at a bizarre resort who are transformed into animals if they fail to find a mate.

His next film, *The Killing of a Sacred Deer*, is one of the creepiest psychological horror films I've ever seen. Barry Keoghan delivers an unforgettable performance as a deeply disturbed young man who terrorizes a family by bestowing a deadly curse upon them. Yorgos drew inspiration for the script from Euripides' tragedy *Iphigenia in Aulis*.

Yorgos began his fruitful collaboration with Emma Stone when he cast her in *The Favourite*, an absurdist satire where she plays an ambitious young lesbian forming a relationship with Queen Anne. In *Poor Things*, Emma portrays a reanimated corpse who becomes a prostitute. The film's provocative nature was so bold that Yorgos immediately started working on another project in case it flopped. His backup film, *Kinds of Kindness*, stars Emma again, this time as a woman willing to slice off her thumb and cook it for her husband. Clearly, Yorgos' idea of romance is at least unconventional.

Yorgos' rehearsal methods are equally unconventional. He incorporates theater games to help the actors bond and loosen up. During the rehearsal of *Poor Things*, Yorgos had the cast roll around on the floor, reciting their dialogue. He would call out one of their names, and they had to jump over the other actors. The next day, actor Ramy Youssef came to him with a note from his doctor saying he couldn't do that anymore.

I won't spoil anything about his new collaboration with Emma Stone. I'm just glad I saw *Bugonia* knowing absolutely nothing. The plot twists were mindblowing.

"There's no wrong or right," Yorgos says of filmmaking. "It's just this thing we put out into the world, and hopefully, each person will be able to experience it in a different way."

Pablo Larraín

I did this sketch at the Los Angeles premiere of *Spencer* at the DGA Theater, where I was struck by Kristen Stewart's powerful performance of Princess Diana. She effectively conveyed the frustration of being trapped in the gilded cage of royalty.

Earlier in his career, Pablo presented a psychopath obsessed with John Travolta in his disturbing Chilean film, *Tony Manero*. In just the first few minutes, the character helps an old woman who has been robbed, takes her back to her apartment, and murders her. Chilling. I was surprised to see a clip from *Grease* in this twisted narrative. The character continues his killing spree by going to a theater showing *Grease* and slamming the projectionist's head into the arc light projector.

This was quite a contrast to his English-language debut, *Jackie*, starring Natalie Portman as Jacqueline Kennedy. Portman's exceptional performance earned her an Oscar nomination. In that movie, he cast my friend, Danish actor Caspar Phillipson, as John F. Kennedy. I was so impressed by Caspar's portrayal that I recruited him for a short, *The Speech That JFK Never Gave* (available on YouTube).

Caspar reprised his Kennedy role in Pablo's third biopic about tragic women, *Maria*, focused on opera legend Maria Callas. In one poignant scene, Callas stands fragile and broken before a mirror, surrounded by statues equally fragile and broken. The scene culminates in a surreal, operatic climax where she slowly paces through her apartment singing, accompanied by dozens of violinists. In her imagination, her late lover Onassis appears, elegantly dressed in a tuxedo, listening to her final aria. Pablo develops a distinctive approach, shifting back and forth from color to black and white, to 8mm home movies. He also beautifully portrays the touching relationship between Callas and her devoted butler and maid.

His film *El Conde* was a thinly disguised black comedy satirizing Chilean dictator Augusto Pinochet, reimagining the notorious leader as a vampire. Shot in black and white, it sharply critiques Pinochet's violation of human rights and economic crimes.

Pablo cites Pasolini, Bergman, Herzog, Cassavetes, and—perhaps most surprisingly—Robert Zemeckis' *Back to the Future* as key influences on his cinematic style.

David Lean

I grew up mesmerized by David Lean's epic films.

Lean loved to travel and appreciated shooting in challenging and exotic locations. He spent nearly a year in Ceylon (now Sri Lanka) making *The Bridge on the River Kwai*, with its memorable bridge explosion. He spent nearly two years in the deserts of Jordan and Morocco shooting *Lawrence of Arabia*. The film involved a cast of thousands, including Bedouins who had never seen a movie. During a battle sequence, Lean devised a clever signaling system: one pistol shot meant "start," sending hundreds of camels galloping, and two shots meant "stop." The camels soon learned these signals and would screech to a halt on hearing two shots.

Working with large crowds, he related his technique. He'd explain the scene to the extras, "simmer" them, building excitement, and once they reached a boiling point, he rolled the cameras. The first take always captured the freshest energy. After that, spontaneity ran down with each subsequent take.

After shooting these outdoor epics, he vowed never to return to that "dark hole," the soundstage. However, shooting *Dr. Zhivago* in Moscow's Red Square was impossible, so he rebuilt it on a studio backlot. The film was trashed by the critics, causing Lean to consider retirement—until the box office exploded. Ultimately, it made more money than all his previous films combined.

For *Ryan's Daughter*, his crew built an entire village in a remote area of Ireland. He waited for several weeks for a real hurricane to come to the location and used a spinning glass in front of the lens of a 65 mm camera so whipping rain would be spun away and the storm could be photographed. The most spectacular storm sequence ever filmed.

When I was scouting locations in Fiji for *The Blue Lagoon*, I heard that Lean was also scouting for *The Bounty*. My producer, Richard Franklin, and I spotted him in our hotel lobby and approached him. Upon hearing what we were up to, Lean confessed that *The Blue Lagoon* had been the racy novel of his adolescence, and he had kept a copy of it under his mattress.

Lean had just arrived from Tahiti, where he reported seeing long lines around the block for screenings of *Grease*. "You young guys are ruining it for us old directors."

Sadly, Lean had a fallout with De Laurentiis and was replaced by Roger Donaldson.

Mimi Leder

Mimi is part of a select group of women who've directed big-budget studio films. She built her filmmaking foundation working on her father Paul's low-budget features, learning the craft from the ground up. Her father's guerrilla filmmaking techniques—doing everything with nothing—became invaluable throughout her career.

She was the first woman accepted into the AFI Conservatory, where she specialized in cinematography. After graduation, she began working as a script supervisor, a job she describes as one of the hardest on the set. Early on, Mimi gained valuable insights working with Mike Fenton and Jane Feinberg, the casting directors of *Shampoo*. Watching Hal Ashby and Warren Beatty run their casting sessions became a masterclass for her.

Her first directing opportunity came when Steven Bochco, the creator of *Hill Street Blues*, and Greg Hoblit, the producer-director, saw her short film, *Short Order Dreams*, and offered her an episode of the show. Unfortunately, Bochco and Hoblit left before she got to direct, and the new producer told Mimi she "wasn't qualified." This was devastating, but she pushed on and eventually directed many episodes of acclaimed shows like *ER*, *China Beach*, and *L.A. Law*, among others. She also directed ten TV pilots, seven of which aired. Years later, the producer who fired her even apologized and worked with her—a rare Hollywood moment.

After directing ten TV movies, Mimi finally got her big-screen break when Steven Spielberg hired her to direct *The Peacemaker*, starring George Clooney and Nicole Kidman. She followed it with the sci-fi disaster film *Deep Impact*. I liked the movie, but unfortunately, its release led Paramount to cancel my planned remake of *When Worlds Collide*.

Her next project, *Pay it Forward*, didn't fare well at the box office. While critics praised the performances, many found the story too emotionally manipulative. As a result, Mimi found herself in "movie jail," where she spent nine frustrating years before returning to the big screen with *The Code*, starring Morgan Freeman and Antonio Banderas.

She also directed the inspiring documentary *On the Basis of Sex*, which followed Ruth Bader Ginsburg's journey to become a Supreme Court Justice.

Throughout her career, Mimi has been a supporter of other women directors. She has utilized her position to hire and mentor young filmmakers. Mimi even recruited future DGA president Leslie Linka Glatter to direct *ER*. Clearly, she has a good eye for finding talent.

Claude Lelouch

I did this sketch at the Waterloo Historical Film Festival in Belgium, where Claude was screening his biggest film, *Les uns et les autres*. The three-hour epic follows four families through three generations, shot in the U.S., Russia, France, and Germany. Today, this movie would cost well over 100 million.

Claude has directed over fifty feature films. As a film student at USC, I loved *A Man and a Woman* and particularly admired *And Now My Love*.

I first met Claude at the 1978 Deauville Film Festival during the European premiere of *Grease*. I brought along my one-minute stop-animation short, *Foot Fetish*, to show him. Claude's enthusiasm for cinema reminded me of my old USC classmates—he loved it so much he insisted the programmers screen it before *Grease*. In return, he showed me his short *C'était un rendez-vous*. A breathtaking dash through the empty streets of Paris at dawn. The film ends at Sacré-Cœur, where a beautiful woman greets the driver, no other than Claude himself! That woman, his then-girlfriend, told me she could hear the car's engine roaring across the city, praying there wouldn't be a crash. Since there was no police blocking the streets, the risk was real. Learning this backstory makes the short downright nail-biting.

Critics often gave Claude a hard time, saying he was too romantic and didn't address important issues. His response is simple: "Cinema is not to teach, it's like a playground to experiment."

For Claude's 85th birthday celebration, his sister Martine contacted me and asked me to send a recorded message. My video greeting in broken French ended up being projected at the Palais des Congrès. Yikes!

Claude is an optimist. "When I make a film, it's like raising an army, an army of emotions. I want to concentrate these emotions to make you laugh, to cry, but most importantly to give you goosebumps."

Over the years, Claude has come to my annual luncheon for French directors attending the City of Lights, City of Angels Film Festival in Hollywood. He has even invited me to stay at his home in Normandy, but I have not yet been able to schedule it. It's definitely on my bucket list.

Rob Lieberman

I met Rob when he lived nearby and was married to my friend, the talented actress Marilu Henner. Marilu is one of those people with a photographic memory who can pull up details about any past date. How fun for Rob. At the time, he was already well-known for his remarkable career in directing commercials—nearly two thousand of them. His work earned widespread acclaim, including twenty-nine Clio Awards, and he was twice voted Best Commercial Director by the DGA.

Rob's prolific output delved into different areas. He directed dozens of episodic shows, including an ambitious version of *Titanic* in 1996. His feature films ran the gamut from the emotional family drama *Table for Five*, starring Jon Voight, to the sci-fi drama *Fire in the Sky*, to two hockey comedies, *D3: The Mighty Ducks* and *Breakaway*. He even worked with the legendary Lauren Bacall in *All I Want for Christmas*. On the small screen, he helped launch the first season of *thirtysomething* with my friends Ed Zwick and Marshall Herskowitz. He also ventured into horror with *The Tortured*, a grim story about every parent's nightmare, the kidnapping and murder of their child. The grieving couple decides to take revenge into their own hands, going after the sadistic serial killer. The extremely graphic sequences were hard to watch, but they served the premise. One thing is for sure: as a director, Rob could not be pigeonholed.

Rob once told me, "The most important quality a film director must have is the ability to inspire the people around him. I always tell the crew that I am their biggest fan because, if they do the best work of their lives, I will get all the credit. They usually laugh."

Rob passed away in 2023, but his legacy lives on. His son, Nick, has followed in his footsteps, co-directing the critically acclaimed mockumentary *Theater Camp*—a fitting tribute to Rob's creative spirit.

Richard Linklater

Richard has broken ground in cinema storytelling in several ways. Take his *Before* trilogy of romantic films—*Before Sunrise, Before Sunset,* and *Before Midnight*—where he directed Ethan Hawke and Julie Delpy over a span of eighteen years. Originally, there was no plan for a trilogy, but the success of each film prompted him to continue the story. He took a further gamble with his extraordinary movie *Boyhood*, where he consciously decided to follow a family for twelve years using the same actors. If anything had happened to any of the cast, or if the lead actor, Ellar Coltrane, had gone through a rebellious period, gotten into drugs, or wanted to quit, what would he have done? When Richard introduced me to Ellar during *Boyhood's* awards campaign, I found him to be a grounded young man. Lucky Richard.

I've been impressed by Richard's experimentation with his animated films, *Waking Life, A Scanner Darkly,* and *Apollo 10 ½: A Space Age Childhood.* He first shoots the actors digitally and edits the footage, then hands it off to a team of animators who transform each frame into a series of drawings that are re-photographed, giving the project a distinctive look: real human emotion, but the visuals of an animated movie.

His breakthrough came with the $23,000 indie *Slacker*, a big hit at Sundance that was later selected by the Library of Congress for the National Film Registry.

Richard is also known for discovering a then-unknown Matthew McConaughey in an Austin bar for *Dazed and Confused*. At first, Richard thought Matthew was too good-looking and wanted someone sleazier!

He combined film noir with screwball comedy in *Hit Man*. He pointed out that in the old days, you couldn't "get away with murder," but times have changed, and audiences can accept morally dubious endings today.

Though people always insisted he'd have to move to Los Angeles or New York to launch a directing career, Richard stayed put in Austin, telling himself, "All I really want is to be here, watch movies, and make movies." He has been able to do just that and even founded the Austin Film Society, partly so he'd have a place to watch films.

I'm always eager to see what Richard does next.

Joshua Logan

I once carried a torch for Josh Logan.

This sketch is from memory, and I will explain the torch in a bit.

Logan was a Broadway legend. At one point, he had four hit shows running simultaneously. He was known for getting great performances out of his actors: Marlon Brando in *Sayonara*, William Holden and Kim Novak in *Picnic*, and Marilyn Monroe in *Bus Stop*. He once said Marilyn was "a combination of Greta Garbo and Charlie Chaplin."

At nineteen, Logan traveled to Russia and managed to observe Stanislavski directing opera. He then studied with him for several years, soaking up the Method before it had even crossed the Atlantic.

Logan directed the theatrical and film versions of the musical *South Pacific*. To adapt the play to film, he wanted to experiment with subtle color filters for the musical numbers. He'd asked to shoot each sequence twice—once with filters, once in natural color—but the studio insisted on tinting only, trusting the lab could remove the filters later. What they didn't say was that removal would take three months. By the time Logan saw the previews, it was too late to meet the film's release schedule. The overly saturated tinted sequences didn't work for me or Logan, who joked he wanted to picket every screening with a sign: "I directed it, and I don't like the color either!"

Now about that torch...

During college, I worked as an extra on his movie *Camelot*. Logan was behind schedule on a night shoot at the massive castle set built on the Warner backlot. He was suspended midair on a Chapman crane beside the Panavision camera, orchestrating the scene from above. Down below, Vanessa Redgrave, Richard Harris, dozens of horseback riders, and over a hundred extras—myself included—stood in position, each holding a torch that had to be lit before every take. The flames only lasted about a minute, which meant assistant directors and prop masters had to race around to re-dip and relight them between shots. The sky was turning purple as dawn was about to break, and Logan desperately needed that last shot. One of the extras (not me!) shouted, "Light the torches!" The crew thought it was their cue and scrambled around lighting them. Logan, realizing the cameras weren't rolling, began screaming and kicking his feet like a baby in a highchair. With the scene lost to the rising sun, the shoot had to be rescheduled for the following night. On the bright side, that prank earned all of us an unexpected extra day's pay.

Sidney Lumet

"I'm mad as hell, and I'm not going to take it anymore!"

This famous battle cry from *Network* fits well into today's world. Though back in 1976, it was satire, it predicted so much that we see today.

Sidney's films often questioned authority and focused on America's working class. After five Oscar nominations, he received an honorary Academy Award in 2005.

In film school, I remember being dazzled by the clever cutting pattern he introduced in *The Pawnbroker*: to transition into a flashback, he'd splice in just a few frames of the incoming shot, then keep splicing in more until the memory completely took over. The technique made it feel like the character was truly reliving a traumatic memory. It was so effective, I had to try it in one of my own student films.

He directed over 50 dramas, including *12 Angry Men*, *Serpico*, and *Prince of the City*. I loved his stylish *Murder on the Orient Express* and *Dog Day Afternoon* made 1970s audiences root for a gay bank robber and his transsexual lover—no small feat at the time.

Sidney was a member of the first-ever class at The Actors Studio in New York. He looked back on all the experimentation they were able to explore. "There was nobody around to say no, because nobody knew enough to say no." His acting background gave him the ability to quickly gain the trust and respect of those he directed. Many called him "every actor's dream." Paul Newman nicknamed him Speedy Gonzales because of his tendency to do one or two takes and get everyone home for dinner.

Sidney's book *Making Movies* is considered one of the best on directing. He outlines something that my mentor and teacher, Nina Foch, always insisted: a filmmaker must find the theme and meaning behind each project—otherwise, why pour your life into it? Another tip in common with Nina is to always read a script in one setting, just as you'd watch a movie. *Making Movies* is well worth a reread before any directing gig.

David Lynch

When David was being considered to direct *The Elephant Man*, his producer, my friend Jonathan Sanger, told me he was apprehensive about how Mel Brooks would react to the surreal and sexual elements of David's AFI film *Eraserhead*. After the screening, Mel embraced David and said, "I love you, you're a madman. You're in." He later said, "David is just like Jimmy Stewart if Stewart were born on Mars."

During post-production on *The Elephant Man*, John Hurt's lines were looped for clarity. David chose to use the scratchy tracks with Hurt speaking under layers of makeup. He felt the sound matched how one would hear the character.

David's version of *Dune* got mixed reactions from the critics and the public, but there are images that vividly stick in my head. I can't unsee the sequence where Kenneth McMillan as Baron Harkonnen pulls a plug out of the chest of a young boy and bathes in his blood. Yikes! And who can forget Sting wearing only a jockstrap with wings? When Dino De Laurentiis did not give David final cut, David disowned the movie, especially the extended "Alan Smithee" TV edit.

Another one-of-a-kind twisted sequence is in *Blue Velvet* when Dennis Hopper makes Isabella Rossellini spread her legs, then gets on his knees, inhales some kind of gas, and cries, "Mommy, mommy, Baby wants to fuck!" When the movie premiered at the Montreal Film Festival, David had a memorable moment. He got to dance with Federico Fellini's wife, the great actress, Giulietta Masina.

Three of his films—*Lost Highway*, *Mulholland Drive*, and *Inland Empire*—follow a dream logic and require multiple viewings for most people (including me) to follow. As he puts it, "We live inside a dream, and when we wake up it's a glorious thing."

David was a filmmaker, painter, sculptor, musician, YouTube performance artist, and, above all, an eccentric character. In 2006, he stood on a Hollywood street corner with a live cow and a sign praising Laura Dern's performance in his *Inland Empire*.

"Ideas are beautiful and abstract, and they exist like fish," he once said, "and if you sit quietly, like you're fishing, you will catch ideas."

David's offbeat sensibility is an inspiration. Although I never officially met him, I could see his house from my bedroom window. I had always hoped our paths would cross.

Jonathan Lynn

I sketched Jonathan during a DGA lecture on comedy. As the director of *Clue*, *My Cousin Vinny*, and *Nuns on the Run*, Jonathan knows a lot about the subject.

He started out as an actor in the late '60s, with roles in *Prudence and the Pill*, *The House That Dripped Blood*, and later *Three Men and a Little Lady*.

When he directed his first feature, *Clue*, Jonathan was not intimidated by its star-packed cast—Christopher Lloyd, Madeline Kahn, and Leslie Ann Warren—simply because he was British and had never seen their work. He had written the screenplay but had only directed plays, so he gave himself a crash course in filmmaking. One of the big challenges was shooting a tightly scripted whodunit out of sequence and making sure each actor knew where they stood in the puzzle.

Jonathan also co-wrote the screenplay for the British thriller *The Internecine Project*, starring James Coburn and Lee Grant, and co-created and co-wrote the British TV series *Yes Minister* and *Yes, Prime Minister*.

Asked about how his acting background helped with his writing and directing, he replied, "Many good playwrights have been actors. Being an actor teaches you about having a good entrance and a good exit... and how to write that. It also teaches you to write dialogue that actors can say."

When *Nuns on the Run* was at Warner Bros., the studio wanted to fire him. He turned to his mentor, Peter Guber, who suggested pitching the project elsewhere. Four years later, Jonathan was successful. Afterward, he asked Guber what he wanted in exchange. "Just special thanks to Peter Guber." Unusual in Hollywood.

I have many favorite scenes in *My Cousin Vinny*, written by my friend Dale Launer. Joe Pesci is hysterically funny as a brash New York lawyer in an antagonistic Southern courthouse. The now-classic "two yutes" exchange with Fred Gwynne as the judge actually came out of a real moment between Pesci and the very British Jonathan when they first met at the Mayflower Hotel in London.

Marisa Tomei's Mona Lisa Vito was the ideal comedic counterpoint to Pesci's Vinny—her quick wit and feisty charm landed her an Oscar for Best Supporting Actress.

James Mangold

James began his career at CalArts and later earned his MFA in film at Columbia University. He has explored a wide range of genres, starting with *Heavy*, a quiet character study about an overweight cook. With the support of his mentor Miloš Forman, he dove headfirst into the gritty action of *Cop Land*, wrangling an extraordinary cast, including De Niro, Keitel, Stallone, Liotta, and Robert Patrick.

I used to work with special needs individuals, so I was especially impressed by the authenticity he brought to *Girl, Interrupted*. Angelina Jolie won the Best Supporting Actress Oscar for her performance.

Joaquin Phoenix and Reese Witherspoon channeled Johnny Cash and June Carter for James in *Walk the Line*, both earning Oscar nominations, and Reese, walking off with the award.

James teamed up with Hugh Jackman more than once—first in the time-travel romantic comedy *Kate & Leopold*, and later in the darker, action-packed world of *The Wolverine* and *Logan*.

One of his biggest challenges was stepping into Steven Spielberg's shoes to direct the fifth *Indiana Jones* movie, a task made even more difficult by the pandemic. His idea was to create a heartfelt tribute to the Golden Age of Cinema.

I like the way James once described how he structures his shoot days based on each actor's "cooking time." Some actors come in hot and best in the first few takes of the day. Others need a slow simmer to warm up, and he saves their key moments for later in the day.

James made the bold decision to cast Timothée Chalamet as Bob Dylan in *A Complete Unknown*. When I first heard about it, I thought it wouldn't work. But after seeing the film, I was completely won over. Chalamet spent years mastering the guitar and harmonica, performing all the songs live, and at times sounding almost indistinguishable from Dylan's recordings. It was truly impressive. I watched an interview where Chalamet broke down his obsessive prep process. He's a dedicated, extraordinarily talented actor who's destined for lasting success. While watching the movie, I was trying to figure out how James captured New York City in the '70s so successfully. It was completely convincing.

James deserves a lot of respect for his eclectic and successful career.

Delbert Mann

Elected president of the Directors Guild and holding the office from 1967 to 1971, Delbert was another of the true gentlemen in the movie business.

Before he got behind the camera, Delbert served as a bomber pilot in World War II. Later, he joked that "B-24 pilot training was very good training for sitting in the hot seat of a live television show—you learn to react coolly to emergencies."

He started in New York during the Golden Age of Television, part of that elite club of live TV pioneers that included John Frankenheimer and George Roy Hill. His big leap into film came with the classic feature *Marty*, starring Ernest Borgnine. The movie was a sleeper hit that ended up winning the Palme d'Or at Cannes, plus a handful of Oscars, including Best Picture and Best Director. Not bad for a story about a lonely Bronx butcher.

Delbert followed it with a wide range of features, from heavy dramas like *Separate Tables*, with Burt Lancaster and Deborah Kerr, *Desire Under the Elms*, with Sophia Loren and Tony Perkins, and *The Dark at the Top of the Stairs*, with Robert Preston and Dorothy McGuire, to lighter-fare comedies like *Lover Come Back*, with Doris Day and Rock Hudson, and *That Touch of Mink*, starring Doris Day and Cary Grant. The man had a range.

Eventually, frustrated with the kinds of features being offered, he hesitated before returning to television. But he saw it as a way to get back to projects he was passionate about.

Thanks to his early days as an actor, Delbert had a deep respect for performance. He demanded absolute silence on his sets when the actors were ready to shoot. He was aware of how distracting even someone moving around in an actor's eyeline could be. He was casual and joked at other times, but if a crew member broke this rule, he would erupt in a rage. That would not happen again.

He faced many challenges shooting his TV movie *All Quiet on the Western Front* in communist Czechoslovakia. Looking back, Delbert called it the one film that came out exactly as he had imagined it.

Tom McCarthy

I sketched Tom around the time he launched his controversial and moving film, *Spotlight*. Based on a true story, the movie earned him the Oscar for Best Original Screenplay and a nomination for Best Director. *Spotlight* follows a team of Boston Globe journalists uncovering the shocking abuse of young boys by local priests—and reveals just how deeply the Catholic Church influenced the media and even the government to hide it. Initially, Tom told the reporters he was too busy to direct their story, but they returned a year later and finally convinced him. "Reporters are horrible people to interview," he joked, noting it took many rounds of questioning to fully grasp the details of their complex story.

Tom started his career as an actor, appearing in diverse roles—from films like *Meet the Parents* and *Syriana* to memorable TV roles, including a stint on HBO's acclaimed drama, *The Wire*.

He also co-wrote Pixar's feature *Up*, which I found to be extremely moving and uplifting—another project that landed him an Oscar nomination for Best Original Screenplay.

Reflecting on the movie industry, Tom once quipped, "There are a lot of ways to make money much easier than this. You get into this business because you love to tell stories. If you get in to get rich, you're an idiot."

His independent film *The Station Agent*, which he wrote and directed, presents three oddball loners who collide and form unusual friendships. It's the kind of understated film that benefits from multiple viewings, revealing deeper emotional levels and subtle humor each time.

In *Stillwater*, Tom guided Matt Damon in the characterization of the ultimate redneck. (What a contrast from Damon in Soderbergh's *Behind the Candelabra*). The gripping story was loosely inspired by the Amanda Knox case. The movie generated controversy and strong objections from Knox herself.

"I have to sometimes pinch myself and say, man, what a wonderful opportunity it's been for me to do this again and again and collaborate with people who are so passionate about it.'"

Charles McDougall

Emmy winner Charles McDougall began directing series in the UK, most notably the original *Queer as Folk*, which was remade in America. He relocated to Hollywood, where he directed six episodes of *Sex and the City*. His style and comedic sensibility caught the eye of producers, landing him the pilot of *Desperate Housewives*. The show quickly became a massive hit, running for eight seasons. I got hooked on the show and loved the campy style and distinctive comedic score.

Charles directed the future Duchess of Sussex, Meghan Markle, in the TV movie *Good Behavior*, a quirky drama about a crime family trying to go straight.

After directing the first two episodes of *The Tudors* and the critically praised pilot of *The Good Wife*, Charles was offered directing gigs on some of the top series around, *The Office, Parks and Recreation,* and the dark political drama *House of Cards*.

He also co-wrote and directed the comedy-drama *Ana*, starring Andy Garcia as a weary car salesman who is roped into caring for an eleven-year-old girl whose mother is incarcerated. That young girl was played by up-and-coming actress Dafne Keen, who wowed audiences in *Logan* and has drawn comparisons to a young Natalie Portman.

In an interview with *The Independent*, Charles joked that he could have stayed in England directing TV, but instead chose Hollywood "to see how badly I could fail." He quickly learned humility, realizing directors aren't really the bosses here. You have to negotiate between an army of producers, writers, and executives who all have opinions. As someone who's navigated my own share of Hollywood meetings, I can relate.

He also had to deal with actors' excesses while working in LA. "I have had one actor who wouldn't allow any close-ups to be shot, and I have had one actress who wouldn't come out of her trailer because she was having intercourse with her boyfriend. There's very rarely a dull moment."

Robert Ellis Miller

Robert and his wife, Pola, were great friends of mine. We served together for many years on the Foreign Language Committee of the Academy, sharing not just screenings but laughs, long conversations, and the occasional disagreement over our favorite contenders. I miss them both.

Before making the leap to feature films, Robert directed countless episodes of classic TV series like *Ben Casey*, *Perry Mason*, and *The Millionaire*. I grew up watching his work before I ever met him.

For his first feature, he cast a young Jane Fonda in the romantic comedy *Any Wednesday*. He rounded out the cast with Jason Robards and Dean Jones, both at the top of their game. The film was based on the Broadway hit of the same name that ran for 983 performances. I remember seeing this during my sophomore year at USC. It was the type of romcom that Hollywood was putting out at the time, before the big transition to films aimed at my generation.

Robert had a real gift for drawing out nuanced performances. He guided both Alan Arkin and Sondra Locke to Oscar nominations in *The Heart Is a Lonely Hunter*, based on the bestselling novel by Carson McCullers. Arkin played a deaf-mute who befriends a special needs young man—a tender, restrained performance that still resonates. In *Reuben Reuben*, Tom Conti plays a brilliant but perpetually drunk poet who's saved by the love of a girl, earning him an Oscar nomination for Best Actor.

I liked Robert's original casting sense. He put Goldie Hawn in a fur hat and thick Russian accent for *The Girl from Petrovka* and turned Brooke Shields into comic-strip heroine *Brenda Starr*. He never went with the obvious choice.

Robert was nominated for the Palme d'Or at Cannes for *The Buttercup Chain*, a British drama about two cousins who bring along romantic partners on a summer trip through Europe, only to slowly realize they might be in love with each other. Cousins finding love? Sounds familiar. One critic said, "Robert Ellis Miller has created a spiritual home in some kind of shadow land of Carson McCullers."

As much as I admired Robert's directing style, what I'll always remember most is the kindness he and Pola showed me when I was starting out. After seeing my USC master's thesis film, *Peege*, they went out of their way to set up screenings for their friends and colleagues. That kind of support sticks with you.

George Miller

Before he was orchestrating pyrotechnical guitar duels in post-apocalyptic deserts, George Miller was an emergency room doctor in Australia. He says his time in the E.R. influenced his filmmaking: "Doctors and filmmakers look at other people from every possible point of view, as a whole, at their organs, at their cells, sometimes in autopsies... every perspective is important, like in filmmaking." He also points out that night shooting is similar to being in the E.R., "You don't know what kind of challenges you'll face, you are often sleep deprived, and need to think optimally under pressure."

George used his medical income to fund his first steps into filmmaking. In the early '80s, he met my USC classmate, Richard Franklin, and became part of the "Australian New Wave." Richard introduced George to Australian composer Brian May, who ended up scoring George's explosive debut: *Mad Max*.

In 1979, while I was working on *The Blue Lagoon* (which was co-produced by Richard Franklin), I caught an early screening of *Mad Max*. I was impressed by the raw energy and style George demonstrated in this first film. Later, I heard that when Roman Polanski saw the movie, he called George a "master of the cinema."

Most sequels begin to stale as they are reworked over and over, but George took the concepts and outdid himself: *The Road Warrior, Mad Max Beyond Thunderdome, Mad Max: Fury Road,* and *Furiosa: A Mad Max Saga*. These movies have little dialogue but roar along with staggering action sequences that build along with the emotion. The Academy noticed, too—*Fury Road* hauled in six Oscars.

On casting, George once said: "You know in the first two seconds as they walk through the door. The rest is a question of confirming that first impression. Then you thank the Movie Gods."

George demonstrated his range with *Babe*, a heartwarming family comedy about a talking pig, where he amazed audiences with the first use of CGI lip sync with animals.

He pushed tech further with the Oscar-winning *Happy Feet*. The CGI penguins were guided by motion-captured dancers and actors. Then George took a virtual camera inside the game engine to handpick his shots.

George is a brilliant storyteller, an innovator, and an inspiration.

Vincente Minnelli

Vincente started out as a costume designer on Broadway. Eventually, he moved into movies and was known for directing MGM musicals. One of his finest was the classic *An American in Paris*, featuring my mentor and dear friend Nina Foch. Nina told me that she came down with the flu, and Vincente had to shut down the production for a week. The good news? This unexpected break gave him time to prepare the Black & White Ball sequence, which was a standout.

Some of my favorites include his nine-Oscar-winning musical *Gigi*, and the dramas *Lust for Life*, and *The Bad and the Beautiful*. Each film showcases his elegant staging, fluid camera movements, and seamless blocking of the actors.

Directing his then-wife Judy Garland, Vincente was amazed at her ability to absorb notes, despite the chaos of makeup artists and hair stylists around her. He could give Judy twenty bits of information without knowing if it was sinking in. Then, when the cameras rolled, she incorporated all his notes perfectly.

I experienced Vincente's kindness firsthand when my Master's Thesis film *Peege* screened at the Los Feliz Theater, and I asked George Cukor to come to see it. As we entered the theater, we spotted Vincente coming up the aisle after watching the main feature. George spontaneously invited him to stay for my film. I was quite nervous, but afterward was thrilled that they were both complimentary.

A few years later, I was sent to Rome to "Americanize" a script written by Italians. Vincente was shooting his last film, *A Matter of Time*, starring his daughter Liza. We were both staying at Hotel de la Ville at the top of the Spanish Steps. I spotted him sitting in the lobby in a canary yellow sport jacket, being besieged by two enthusiastic American matrons. I did a quick sketch and then went over to rescue him. I reminded him that we had met in LA, but sadly, he was experiencing the beginnings of Alzheimer's and asked where the car was. He thought I was his driver.

Lin-Manuel Miranda

Lin-Manuel is best known for creating and starring in the groundbreaking musicals *Hamilton* and *In the Heights*. For quite a while, getting tickets to *Hamilton* was a major accomplishment. The musical quickly became a part of American pop culture, sweeping up eight Drama Desk Awards, seven Olivier Awards, eleven Tony Awards, a Grammy, and a Pulitzer Prize. In 2018, his extraordinary contributions to culture earned him the prestigious Kennedy Center Honors.

Lin-Manuel's passion for directing took root early—at the age of three, while he spent days knocking around his grandfather's VHS video store in Puerto Rico, aptly named Miranda Video.

I first met him at a screening of his directorial debut film, *tick, tick... BOOM!*, adapted from the semi-autobiographical play of the same name written by Jonathan Larson. Lin-Manuel had seen the off-Broadway show at age twenty-one and immediately knew on a bone-deep level that he wanted to someday bring it to the big screen.

One remarkable aspect of the film was casting Andrew Garfield as the lead, despite his lack of professional singing experience. Andrew was apprehensive and especially worried about performing an a cappella number—originally sung solo by Larson himself at the start of the play. Lin-Manuel cleverly repositioned this pivotal song at a birthday party scene, guiding Andrew to areas around the apartment to create the illusion of "improvised" lyrics. With patience and careful rehearsal, Lin-Manuel enabled Andrew to deliver a performance so authentic and powerful it seemed he'd been belting Broadway numbers his entire life.

The cast included several Broadway performers who had personally worked with Jonathan Larson, making the film a true tribute to his legacy. Lin-Manuel remarked, "This is a movie about failure, about getting back up. His masterpiece is ahead of him, and it's hopeful because maybe so is yours."

Showing off even more of his creative range, Lin-Manuel took on the Dick Van Dyke role in *Mary Poppins Returns*, voiced *Vivo* the charming kinkajou (and wrote songs!) for the animated feature *Vivo*, and penned the catchy, Oscar-nominated tunes for Disney's hits *Encanto* and *Moana*. He wrote more songs for *Moana 2*, *The Little Mermaid*, *Mufasa: The Lion King*, and worked on the music for two *Star Wars* movies.

Looking back on the night I met Lin-Manuel, I enjoyed chatting with him. For someone so accomplished, I found him to be very down-to-earth.

Paul Morrissey

I screwed up the sound on Paul Morrissey's *Heat*.

Well, just one take. In 1971, he was shooting the Warhol production at the Tropicana Motel in West Hollywood. I met Paul in one of the rooms where he was holed up with the script. Meanwhile, the crew was already filming out by the pool. Shooting without the director? Odd, but it was a Warhol production. Pat Ast and Joe Dallesandro were improvising a scene, while Andy Warhol's boyfriend, Jed Johnson, was running the camera. (It's still hard to believe Jed was lost in the TWA Flight 800 crash—such a tragedy.) The sound guy had wandered off, and Jed turned to me: "Do you know how to run a Nagra?" "Of course," I lied, channeling my recent USC grad confidence. I'd never touched one. I fumbled with it and managed to erase a take. After being yelled at, I quietly slinked away. The next day, I ran into Paul and Jed at the Frank Lloyd Wright home of James Bridges and Jack Larson. Jed had forgiven me, and Paul hadn't even noticed.

Paul's first film, *Chelsea Girls*, had no plot—just two side-by-side projections, sometimes shown out of order. I enjoyed his campy horror films *Flesh for Frankenstein* and *Blood for Dracula*. Paul often cast trans women, which was revolutionary back then. His reasoning was totally blunt, "They were funny, interesting, and different—and I loved them."

Later on, he tried more mainstream films like *The Hound of the Baskervilles* with Dudley Moore and Peter Cook, and *Spike of Bensonhurst* with Ernest Borgnine. He also managed The Velvet Underground, though producing their first album wasn't easy. "They were stupid and didn't know what they were doing. After their first record, I don't think they ever made a tune you could listen to."

But it was his relationship with Warhol that define him. Paul always bristled at the "Andy Warhol Presents" credit. "Andy didn't know how to do anything except take all the credit. I was the driving force. For fifty years, I've had to live with people saying, 'It's Warhol this,' or 'He did them with me.' Forget it. He was incompetent—anorexic, illiterate, autistic, Asperger's. He never did a thing in his entire life. He sort of wandered through it like a zombie, and somehow, that worked for him."

Whatever went on behind the Factory doors, Paul was a fascinating figure in filmmaking. Someone you didn't forget—especially if you once *accidentally* erased his audio.

Jonathan Mostow

Back in 1996, Jonathan was all set to direct a movie called *Stephen King's Trucks*—until lawyers said that they couldn't use King's name in the title. The film was nearly scrapped, but Jonathan, showing the kind of quick thinking you need in this business, dove in, rewrote it, and saved the project. He also kept it manageable: mostly exteriors with minimal location permit hassles. Smart move for a director starting out. That project evolved into *Breakdown*, a simple, terrifying premise: your car breaks down in the middle of nowhere, your wife vanishes, and you're left scrambling. Jonathan created great action sequences. For a nail-biting scene with a truck and a car dangling off a bridge, he ditched the easy VFX route. He shot it real, which was more expensive and dangerous, but Jonathan fought for it, and it worked.

Breakdown was a hit and led to action movies like *U-571* and the reboot of the *Terminator* franchise, *Terminator 3: Rise of the Machines*. The stakes were high, and Jonathan was understandably nervous about showing *Terminator* to James Cameron. Jonathan originally cast Sophia Bush in a key role, but as production went on, it became clear that she looked too young for the part and had to replaced her with Claire Danes. The decision broke his heart—he'd really wanted to give Sophia her big break, recognizing her talent.

My brother Jeff, a visual effects artist, worked with Jonathan on *Surrogates*, creating a younger avatar of Bruce Willis. It was cutting-edge stuff back then, building on techniques pioneered in *The Curious Case of Benjamin Button*. With new AI advancements, digital de-aging may soon become a standard request in actors' contracts.

I agree with Jonathan's take on many blockbuster CGI action pictures: a firehose of visual effects blasting you in the face. He adds they often suffer from a "flabby narrative."

Jonathan is very involved at the Directors Guild, where he co-chairs the Creative Rights Committee with Christopher Nolan. They do crucial work. Before COVID changed everything, they got studios to commit to more "in-person" casting, not just relying on tapes. That committee has pushed through many key improvements for directors' rights.

Jonathan says every director needs more time and money. "Whatever resources you're given, you're always trying to push the envelope. There's no prize you get when you come back to the studio at the end and say, 'Here's your refund of what we didn't spend.'"

Phillip Noyce

Phillip began making low-budget, stylish films in Australia. One of them, *Newsfront*, was shot by Vincent Monton, who told me about a clever solution Phillip came up with for a scene where a reporter rows a boat down a flooded town street. Instead of building a fake town and flooding it, he built just the top halves of building facades in an actual river. Simple and effective. Vincent and I had a good laugh picturing some Hollywood producer insisting on submerging an entire backlot town.

Phillip also directed the gripping Australian thriller, *Dead Calm*. I recall seeing this when it came out in '89. Sam Neill and a very young Nicole Kidman play a couple on a sailboat trip when Billy Zane rows up from an abandoned boat, claiming everyone on board died from food poisoning. The tension ramps up and up as you realize this guy is bad news. That film put Nicole on the map and got Hollywood calling Phillip, too. He moved into big-budget features like *Patriot Games and Clear* and *Present Danger* with Harrison Ford, and *The Bone Collector* with Denzel Washington and Angelina Jolie. His biggest box office smash was *Salt*, again with Angelina, pulling in nearly $300 million. However, he was stunned by how the studios could "hypnotize the audiences all over the world to see the movies, guaranteeing the movies were a success whether they were good, bad, or indifferent."

Phillip had a rough time on *Sliver*. He was quitting smoking, had a slow cameraman, leads that didn't get along, and a producer who didn't want him. My mentor Nina Foch was in it, playing a woman secretly watched by hidden cameras. At one point, there was a bizarre idea to reveal she was a man—she'd lather up her face with shaving cream. She was relieved when the idea was abandoned.

In Hollywood, Phillip sometimes felt like a gun for hire. So he took a short breather from the studio machine and headed back to Australia to direct the powerful drama, *Rabbit-Proof Fence*, a true story about the heartbreaking government policy that tore Aboriginal kids from their families. He cast mostly first-time kids who'd literally never seen a movie camera before, and somehow got performances so raw and honest that it feels like you're watching a documentary.

He followed up with the drama, *The Quiet American*, starring Michael Caine and Brendan Fraser in a love triangle with a beautiful local Vietnamese girl.

"A director has to have a hard back and a soft front. Hard back because everyone around you has to believe you're going to go forward...a soft front because everyone must feel they can say anything and you'll accept it."

Kenny Ortega

Kenny has had a jam-packed and varied career. He started out as an actor in musical theater, then moved to choreography, working with Gene Kelly and my friend Olivia Newton-John on *Xanadu*. He studied choreography with his mentor Gene Kelly as part of Francis Ford Copolla's American Zoetrope Studios experiment.

Then the '80s hit, and Kenny's choreography was everywhere. He connected with John Hughes to work on *Pretty in Pink* and *Ferris Bueller's Day Off*, but the choreography everyone still talks about was in *Dirty Dancing*: the famous moment when Patrick Swayze lifted Jennifer "Baby" Grey.

In the live performance arena, Kenny choreographed the famous music video, "If I Could Turn Back Time," with Cher on an aircraft carrier with hundreds of sailors. He also spearheaded concert tours for Gloria Estefan and KISS, showing quite a range. He's tackled the Super Bowl halftime show, the Academy Awards, and both the Summer and Winter Olympics. And remember Madonna's hit "Material Girl" channeling Marilyn Monroe's "Diamonds Are a Girl's Best Friend"? That was Kenny, too.

It was only a matter of time before he turned to directing. His first feature was Disney's original musical, *Newsies*, starring a young Christian Bale. Continuing at Disney, he directed Bette Midler, Kathy Najimy, and Sarah Jessica Parker as witches in the comedy *Hocus Pocus*. Later on, he conquered a whole generation of kids with the *High School Musical* phenomenon.

It makes me smile to hear that when Kenny is directing, if anyone yawns on the set, he makes them pay a dollar into a fund that he gives to the Make-A-Wish Foundation at the end of the shoot.

Kenny had a long association with Michael Jackson, creating and designing two world tours, "Dangerous" and "HIStory." He was working on Michael's huge comeback tour entitled "This Is It" when Michael suddenly died. Less than two weeks later, Kenny directed the memorial service for Michael at the Staples Center on the very stage where they had been rehearsing the tour. In his moving eulogy, he spoke about the venue being Michael's house and the artists being his family. Later, Kenny pieced together footage from rehearsals to make the poignant documentary *This Is It*.

Kenny has won three Emmys and has a star on the Hollywood Walk of Fame. It all started with a kid who was a cheerleader at Sequoia High School in Redwood City, California. Not bad.

Daniel Petrie

Canadian Dan Petrie Sr. was a real workhorse who started way back in the Golden Age of Television in the '50s. He ended up directing over ninety films and television programs. It's a long list. He is best known for *A Raisin in the Sun*. The film starred Sidney Poitier and Louis Gossett Jr. and dealt with the struggles of an African-American family trying to make a better life.

Dan was also a master of TV movies back when they were major cultural events. His *Eleanor and Franklin* and *Eleanor and Franklin: The White House Years*, starring Ed Herrmann and Jane Alexander, swept the Emmys with 18 awards.

One of his films that always stuck with me, maybe a bit under the radar, is *Lifeguard*, starring Sam Elliott and Anne Archer. It's about an aging lifeguard who faces growing pains in a moving way. Another is *The Betsy*, with Laurence Olivier, no less, as an automobile tycoon trying to develop a fuel-efficient car.

Dan worked with many heavy hitters. He directed the gritty *Fort Apache, The Bronx* with Paul Newman and Ed Asner. *My Name is Bill W.* had James Woods giving a powerhouse performance as the Alcoholics Anonymous co-founder. He also guided Sally Field to an Emmy for her harrowing role as *Sybil*.

"Happiness is going toward a soundstage with Jane Fonda in it." Dan directed Jane in *The Dollmaker* and admired her dedication as an actor. For the role, she lived for several weeks in Tennessee doing research and picked up the accent, then she used it throughout the shoot, even off camera.

During his early television days, he dealt with the blacklisting of actors. He hired Martin Ritt, who later became a fine director himself, and Madeleine Sherwood in two separate productions, only to have the network suits force him to fire them because of their left-leaning views.

When video villages came in, Dan was swept up in the technology until George C. Scott reminded him that the director is an audience of one for the actor. Scott wanted him to be by the camera, watching him up close. Dan returned to his original technique of sitting right by the camera.

Dan Sr. was also patriarch to a showbiz dynasty. His wife, Dorothea, was an Emmy-winning producer for *Love is Never Silent*, and *Caroline?* His son, Don, directed the big comedy hits *How to Lose a Guy in 10 Days* and *Miss Congeniality*. And his other son, Dan Jr., wrote *Beverly Hills Cop* and served as president of the Writers Guild.

As far as I'm concerned, the Petrie clan is Hollywood royalty.

Donald Petrie

Don, the son of Daniel and Dorothea Petrie and brother of Daniel Jr., grew up in a household where directing was the family business. His father was both mentor and gateway, getting Don his first gigs as a production assistant.

One early opportunity had him driving Sir Laurence Olivier. Unsure how to address a living legend, Don asked, "Should I call you Lord or Your Highness?" Olivier replied, "Call me Larry." Soon, Don was running lines with him and shared a funny memory: as a boy, Don once saw a poster for *Othello*, featuring Olivier in blackface. For years, he assumed Olivier was African American.

Don studied theater at California State University, Northridge, and later became a Fellow at the American Film Institute. His feature directorial debut came in 1988 with *Mystic Pizza*, where he introduced the world to a young Julia Roberts. He went on to become a go-to guy for feel-good hits like *Grumpy Old Men, How to Lose a Guy in 10 Days*, and *Miss Congeniality*. He continued his romcom streak by shooting *The Last Resort* in the Philippines.

In 2002, Don and I did a videoconference from the DGA to students at Vanderbilt University as part of the Video Outreach program. Don was refreshingly honest, admitting that he looks back at his AFI student films and sees the mistakes. But, as he said, film school lets you fail without killing your career. He emphasized communication skills, encouraged studying psychology—"you'll need it working with actors"—and reminded them that sometimes the best film school is just living life and finding stories to tell.

Don gave a great practical mantra, the nine P's: Proper Pre Production Planning Prevents Piss Poor Post Production. A little crude but completely true. He also joked that some people say continuity is for sissies. If the story is working, viewers rarely notice mismatches.

Using film clips, Don broke down directing techniques: how tight eyelines create intimacy while wide eyelines create distance, or how cross-cutting can keep the story interesting and fast-paced. He even explained Sandra Bullock's transformation in *Miss Congeniality*, starting with wide, unflattering lenses, then gradually shifting to longer lenses and refined makeup as her character blossomed. The students were transfixed by Don's ability to convey complex concepts, and I was very impressed by his teaching skills.

Beyond directing, Don has been a stand-up guy at the Directors Guild, hosting tennis tournaments, moderating panels, and always helping fellow directors. He carries on the Petrie tradition.

William Phelps

Andy Warhol screen-tested Bill Phelps in 1965. He was then known as Buffy and part of the Factory scene in New York. Bill's father, concerned about Warhol's influence, persuaded him to move to California and enroll at USC film school, where I met him. Warhol's influence remained. One infamous moment came when the head of the film school, Bernie Kantor, led a tour group into the soundstage and found Bill naked, strapped to a cross, being whipped for an avant-garde film he was making.

Bill eventually settled down, and we collaborated on several student films, including my thesis *hands in innocence*. He brought a film noir look to the story of a special-needs girl returning home from a mental hospital.

When I saw Bill's documentary *Wave Warriors* about the surfers of Oahu's famous North Shore, I saw potential for a dramatic narrative film. Since I owned a beach house there, I invited Bill to research the culture and conflicts between local Hawaiian surfers and mainlanders. Together, we developed the concept of a young surfer from an Arizona wave tank trying to integrate into Hawaii's surf scene. We pitched the idea to Tom Pollock at Universal, who greenlit the project immediately.

The result was *North Shore*, directed by Bill, and now seen by surfers worldwide. Many fans can quote its iconic lines, such as "When the wave breaks here, don't be there" and "You're so haole you don't even know you're haole." Anniversary screenings consistently draw packed audiences of surfers and fans.

For authenticity, we cast real surfers like Gerry Lopez and Laird Hamilton in supporting roles. For the lead roles, we needed actors who could surf. While Josh Brolin was too old for the lead and too young for the guru role, Gregory Harrison and Matt Adler fit perfectly. For Turtle, the quirky surf rat, I championed John Philbin, who had impressed me in my movie *Grandview, USA*. Initially overweight and pale, John transformed himself in Hawaii into a ripped, tan surfer with a convincing pidgin accent. His portrayal of the goofy, lovable court jester and surfboard sander became a cult favorite among surfers.

Bill and I have spent years developing ideas for a sequel, hoping to reunite the original cast with a new generation of surfers. Sadly, we've received no support from Universal for the project.

Jeremy Podeswa

Canadian filmmaker Jeremy Podeswa started out making his own short films and indie features—exactly the kind of fresh, edgy voice the producers of the American version of *Queer As Folk* were looking for. The series, shot in Canada, needed a bold and authentic take on gay life, and Jeremy delivered. His direction was unapologetic and realistic, and he was given free rein to experiment. He used split-screen moving boxes, reminiscent of *The Thomas Crown Affair*, and at one point, shot in black and white with still images, evoking *Raging Bull*. The series broke ground with its graphic portrayal of homosexuality, and Jeremy was proud to be part of it. It wasn't just TV; it changed public perception, and perhaps, inspired young gay people to feel better about themselves.

After shooting *Queer As Folk*, Jeremy received a call from Alan Poul, a producer at HBO. Jeremy's earlier indie feature, *The Five Senses*, had impressed Alan, and he invited him to the States to direct *Six Feet Under*. This opened the door to a slew of prestige television work, including *Carnivàle*, *Boardwalk Empire*, and *The Handmaid's Tale*.

When HBO sent him to Italy to shoot an episode of *Rome*, the stakes skyrocketed. It was the biggest show on television at the time, ten million dollars an hour. Jeremy admitted to a moment of panic (who wouldn't?), but quickly came to the realization that I think most directors eventually come to: directing is directing. Doesn't matter if you're shooting on a shoestring or in the Roman Colosseum; the job is to take the scene and make it work. He later said he wished everyone he'd ever known could have seen him high on a crane at the giant Cinecittà Studios set, directing hundreds of period extras.

Game of Thrones was even bigger. Juggling locations in multiple countries, tons of visual effects, and a huge ensemble cast. Plus, trying to be as creative as possible while fulfilling the showrunners' vision. Something every director working in TV faces. Lately, he has become a go-to for sci-fi projects, directing the series *Station Eleven*, *3 Body Problem*, and *Blade Runner 2099*.

Jeremy is also committed to mentoring up-and-coming filmmakers. He remembers how much it meant to him to be inspired by professionals when starting out.

"Before I block a scene, I look at the set from all angles, standing on a chair, lying on the floor. Where are the entrances and exits? Then I read the scene from each character's point of view to get an idea where they might move."

Roman Polanski

I saw Roman Polanski's first film, *Knife in the Water*, while I was in film school. I was struck by his distinctive style. I remember the lead character lying on the boat in a Christlike pose, shot from high above the mast. That image stuck with me. Then came *Repulsion*. I'll never forget the jolt I got when a figure suddenly appeared in the mirrored medicine cabinet door as it swung shut. I rewatched the film recently and, again, my heart skipped a beat. I'm a fan of his films, *Rosemary's Baby* and *Chinatown*, both considered classics.

The first time I saw Roman in person was back in 1966, on the Malibu set of *Don't Make Waves*, where he was visiting his wife, Sharon Tate. I was just a surfer extra, but I remember two things vividly: how affectionate they were with each other, and how pale her skin was. Each day, the crew covered her in tan pancake makeup.

Three years later, like everyone else around the world, I was horrified by Sharon's murder by the Manson clan. At the time, I happened to be renting a room from George Lucas, not far from the Benedict Canyon crime scene. Roman later dedicated his film *Tess* to Sharon, whom he had hoped to cast in the lead.

In 2009, Roman was invited to accept an award at the Zürich Film Festival. Debra Winger and I were on the festival jury and were scheduled to have dinner with him that night. The audience was already seated in the theater, waiting for his appearance, but he didn't show. He'd been arrested at the airport, at the request of United States authorities. That night, the festival programmer ran *Roman Polanski: Wanted and Desired*, a documentary exploring alleged judicial misconduct in his 1977 sentencing for unlawful sex with a minor. Roman was placed under house arrest and, a year later, was released by the Swiss government.

In 2019, I was dining at an outdoor café in Paris with my friend Alejandra Norambuena, the executive director of the Franco-American Cultural Fund. She spotted Roman and called him over to our table. Just like that, five decades after I first saw him, we finally met.

Otto Preminger

Otto Preminger mistook me for a gigolo—but more on that in a bit.

Otto was the cinematic mind behind the classic film noir, *Laura*, with its lush score by David Raksin. He tackled taboo topics head-on: drug addiction in *The Man with the Golden Arm*, rape in *Anatomy of a Murder*, and homosexuality within Washington politics in *Advise & Consent*. His films broke censorship ground, being the first to mention "virgin," "pregnant," "rape," "sperm," and "sexual climax."

Twice nominated for an Academy Award for Best Director, Otto also found himself cast as the quintessential villain—mostly as a Nazi, thanks to his imposing look and German accent. He was so believable on the set of *Stalag 17* that director Billy Wilder joked, "I must be nice to you because I have family in Germany."

Otto wanted to be an actor from age nine. By twenty-one, he had started his own theater in Vienna. When he moved into film, Otto didn't care about making money. He was just happy he didn't have to do the same thing from nine to five.

Novelist Leon Uris wasn't thrilled with Otto's screen adaptation of *Exodus*. Otto, who had hired Leon to write the screenplay, wasn't happy with him either. His philosophy was that if he had bought the book, he was the owner and had no obligation to be faithful to it. He focused on the part of the story that interested him and hired blacklisted writer Dalton Trumbo to write the draft that was filmed.

He had a rough time directing Marilyn Monroe on *River of No Return*. "She could never be on time. Even when she was there, she was late." He said she had no talent as an actress, but once the camera was on her, she was a true movie star.

Otto was known as a bully, but I didn't see any indication of this when I met him in 1971. My mentor Nina Foch invited me to the New York City set of *Such Good Friends*, where she was playing Dyan Cannon's mother. I was right out of film school, 25 and blond. When Nina introduced me to Preminger, he took one look at me, then winked at Nina, assuming I was her boy toy.

Irving Rapper

Irving directed one of the most famous romantic scenes in cinema. You know the one—from *Now, Voyager*, where Paul Henreid lights two cigarettes in his mouth and hands one to Bette Davis. Max Steiner's lush score soars as Bette delivers that immortal line, "Don't let's ask for the moon. We have the stars." Hard to top that.

Irving teamed up with Bette in several more films, including *Dark Victory, The Corn Is Green,* and *Deception*. His working relationship with her was strained at times. An example: the ending of *Deception* was supposed to be upbeat, but Bette insisted her character should shoot Claude Rains' character dead. Irving, picking his battles, let Bette have her way. It's possible Bette thought Claude was stealing the show and wanted the final word—literally.

I met Irving at a soiree at my good friend George Cukor's home when I was a student at USC. After watching some of my student films, Irving offered some pointers and career advice.

Although his film *One Foot in Heaven* was nominated for Best Picture in 1941, Irving told me his personal favorite was *The Brave One*. It's an extremely moving picture about a Mexican boy and his pet bull that ends up facing a top matador. Dalton Trumbo won an Oscar for the screenplay, but he had to use the pseudonym Robert Rich due to the blacklist. It wasn't until 19 years later that the Academy reissued the Oscar to Trumbo.

While Irving made plenty of love stories, he also ventured into other genres—including two "sword and sandal" epics in Europe, *Constantine and the Cross,* and *Pontius Pilate*. And in 1950, he directed the first film version of Tennessee Williams' classic *The Glass Menagerie*, starring Jane Wyman and Kirk Douglas.

In 1970, Irving made another surprising genre shift with *The Christine Jorgensen Story*, one of the first mainstream features to focus on a transgender character. My USC classmate, Howard Kazanjian, worked as the AD and filled me in on some details. Apparently, Irving demanded absolute silence on the set. If an actor blew a line, Irving would dress them down in a quiet but articulate rant. Howard also mentioned that the real Christine Jorgensen was often on the set, having her hair combed over by the picture's hairdresser. That year, Irving took Christine Jorgensen to the Oscars as his date. Quite a progressive statement for 1970.

Irving spent his final years at the Motion Picture & Television Fund home in Woodland Hills, where he passed in 1999 at age 101.

Peyton Reed

Peyton directed two episodes of my favorite series, *The Mandalorian*.

He began his directing career creating "making-of" documentaries for *Back to the Future* and *Forrest Gump*. He also, funnily enough, directed the preshow for the Disney Theme Park attraction I directed, *Honey, I Shrunk the Audience*. After various TV assignments, Peyton made the leap to features with *Bring It On*, which became a sleeper hit. He carved out a niche in comedy with *Down with Love*, starring Ewan McGregor and Renée Zellweger, *Yes Man* with Jim Carrey, and *The Break-Up* with Jennifer Aniston and his future *Mandalorian* producer Jon Favreau. It was Jon who later invited Peyton to direct an episode of *The Mandalorian*, giving him the chance to work in "The Volume"—a giant LED screen that allows real-time compositing. He found this great research for *Ant-Man and the Wasp: Quantumania*, the last film in his *Ant-Man* trilogy for Marvel. A self-proclaimed sci-fi nerd, he was thrilled to get the assignment. He was a comic book fan and managed to bring a layer of comedy into the franchise. "In terms of the public consciousness, Ant-Man was a B-level, maybe a C-level character. I love that about him."

Peyton's interest in movies began when he saw the original *Planet of the Apes*. "I loved the ape makeup. The movie really has a lot to say about race, about the uneasy alliance between science and religion, and about evolution. It's such a smart movie." He says it's one of those films that grows with you as you get older. Another early favorite was *Paper Moon*. He was the same age as Tatum O'Neal when he saw it, and it made a strong impression.

As he got deeper into cinema, one movie that stood out above the rest was Francois Truffaut's *The 400 Blows*. He even owns a 16mm print. It was the first of five movies starring Jean-Pierre Léaud as Truffaut's cinematic alter ego. I'm a fan of these films too—there's something fascinating about watching a character grow up on-screen. In a way, they were a precursor to what Richard Linklater achieved decades later with *Boyhood*.

One of Peyton's favorite pieces of directing advice comes from British director Ronald Neame. Neame was directing Alec Guinness when he told him, "You're not praising me enough." Neame, surprised, protested that he never thought he had to praise Alec Guinness, a legendary actor who clearly knows what he is doing. Guinness then told him, "My boy, if you expect to have a career making movies, there's one thing you have to remember: All actors are twelve-year-olds at heart, and they have to be praised."

Carl Reiner

I had the honor of conducting Carl's Visual History interview for the Directors Guild Archives. When I asked if he ever gave actors line readings, he said, "I don't like to give actors line readings unless it's so off that they're killing a joke. Then I take them to the dressing room and ask to go over the scene. I'll suggest putting the accent on the proper word. If they don't get it, I'll show them." A smart way to handle it without exposing the actor in front of the whole crew.

Carl was a multi-award-winning icon who got his start in the early days of television, writing sketches with Sid Caesar, Mel Brooks, Neil Simon, and Woody Allen. Not a bad company. He went on to create *The Dick Van Dyke Show* and made his mark as both actor and director, helming feature comedies like *The Jerk, Where's Poppa?, Oh, God!,* and *All of Me*.

He was one of the funniest people I've ever met. We served on the Academy's Screening Committee with Nina Foch, and Carl would always regale us with jokes to lighten up the sessions. Here's a classic: An old man is assigned a new nurse for a day. She pays close attention to him, and every time she sees him tilting over in his chair, she straightens him up. At the end of the day, someone asked the old man what he thought of the nurse. "She was very pretty, but didn't allow me to fart."

Carl directed Mickey Rooney in *The Comic* and wanted him to look like silent film star Ben Turpin, known for his exaggerated crossed eyes. Mickey couldn't do it, so he had to use a special contact lens which could only be worn for thirty seconds at a time. Nothing's easy.

Some actors just don't get satire. Carl directed a film noir spoof and told his actor to cross a room with a "cool" attitude. The actor bobbed his head like a modern hipster, convinced that it was cool. Carl tried a different approach. He told him to walk like he was passing through a woman's shower full of naked women and not allowed to react. No luck. He then told the actor to imagine a rod running from the top of his head to his feet. That finally did the trick, but it was long and painful.

Carl and I chatted for three hours about his extraordinary career, and I spent much of that time laughing. He was one of a kind.

You can find a link to my interview with Carl at www.randalkleiser.com

Gene Reynolds

As a film student in 1967, I worked in the Screen Extras Guild and landed a gig as a stand-in on a TV show called *Love On A Rooftop*, directed by Gene Reynolds. He was receptive to my endless barrage of questions about the film industry. His perspective as a working professional was the perfect complement to what I was learning at USC, where the professors focused mostly on the basics and theory.

Gene began his career in front of the camera. "I was discovered in my living room by my mother." Gene was an extra in *Babes in Toyland* with Laurel and Hardy and in the *Our Gang* comedies. As a child actor, he landed roles in *Captains Courageous* and *Santa Fe Trail*, and was often cast as the younger version of stars like James Stewart, Robert Taylor, Don Ameche, and Tyrone Power. One of his biggest roles was in *Boys Town*, where he cried in Spencer Tracy's arms.

After acting in 80 films and TV series, including *I Love Lucy* and *Hallmark Hall of Fame*, Gene grew tired of waiting for the phone to ring and decided to shift gears. He jumped into casting, which eventually led to directing—a move that skyrocketed his career. He directed scores of popular TV shows of the period, such as *Hogan's Heroes, Gidget, My Three Sons, The Munsters, The Andy Griffith Show*, and *Room 222*. But his biggest claim to fame was co-creating the TV series, M*A*S*H. As an executive producer, he oversaw 120 episodes, often directing them. The New York Times fittingly called him "the architect of M*A*S*H." Gene also spearheaded the series *Lou Grant* and racked up 6 Emmys during his career.

In 1993, Gene was elected president of the Directors Guild, serving for four years. By then, I was a Guild member, and Gene recruited me to produce a documentary with him, *Directing: How to Get There*. We asked top directors to share advice for young filmmakers starting out.

Gene was the reason I got involved with the Guild, eventually serving on the National Board and several committees, including our annual Digital Day, which I helped program for over 20 years.

John Rich

In the fall of 1964, fresh off the plane from the East Coast and newly arrived on the USC campus, I saw a TV crew filming a show by the library. Without thinking, I jumped at the chance and joined the background extras, doing crosses behind the principals, trying my best to look like I belonged there. I was soon discovered by John Rich's assistant director and kicked off the set.

Undeterred, I joined the Screen Extras Guild and later returned as a paid extra on John's film *Easy Come, Easy Go*. Watching him guide Elvis Presley through musical numbers turned out to be invaluable training, especially years later, when I worked with John Travolta on *Grease*.

This was long before IMDb, so I had no idea at the time that John Rich was behind so many television shows I had watched growing up. *Mister Ed, That Girl, The Brady Bunch, Gomer Pyle: USMC, Gunsmoke, Hogan's Heroes, Bonanza,* and *Gilligan's Island*—he'd directed them all. It was his show, *Our Miss Brooks*, that gave me the inspiration to cast Eve Arden as Principal McGee in *Grease*.

John became hugely successful directing classic sitcoms, especially during his long run on *All in the Family*, where he earned two well-deserved Emmys. One of the biggest laughs he ever got came in an episode featuring Sammy Davis, Jr., playing himself. In the scene, Sammy stops by Archie Bunker's house to retrieve a briefcase he left in Archie's cab. Before leaving, Sammy thanks the narrow-minded Archie with a kiss. The laugh lasted so long that John had to trim it for the final broadcast. Television history.

John picked up another Emmy earlier in his career for directing some of the foundational episodes of Carl Reiner's brilliant *The Dick Van Dyke Show*.

Later on, John partnered up with Henry Winkler ('The Fonz' himself!) to form a production company, and together they produced the adventure series *MacGyver*.

At meetings of the Western Directors' Council, John always had a joke ready when there was a lull in the agenda. He was also a stickler for spelling and punctuation, and studied the meeting minutes obsessively. He never failed to find something to correct, usually down to the smallest detail.

I was both surprised and honored when John stood up at a DGA National Board meeting and nominated me for membership. He never knew that I once snuck onto his set.

Guy Ritchie

I first became aware of Guy in 1998 when I saw his stylish debut, *Lock, Stock and Two Smoking Barrels*. It was fast, funny, gritty, and completely original. I was hooked. Then came *Snatch*, *RocknRolla*, and *The Gentlemen*. In all four films, Guy plays with converging plotlines, snappy and snarky narration, and that signature mix of humor and violence. He often uses split screens, speed ramps, quick cuts, and title sequences that punch you in the face—in a good way. His style is loud, visual, and instantly recognizable.

His gangster films became so well known that actual gangsters began approaching him, wanting their own nefarious and nasty stories turned into one of Guy's movies. I don't know if I would have been flattered or scared.

Actors have revealed that Guy keeps them on their toes. He's known for sometimes throwing out the planned scene for the day and coming up with an entirely new one.

I'm probably not the only person to say that his one miss was the remake of *Swept Away*, starring his then-wife, Madonna. The film won five Golden Raspberry Awards. Ouch!

I sketched him at the Producers Guild screening of *Sherlock Holmes* in 2009. The first time Guy saw the fully completed film. Robert Downey Jr. was also in the audience, seeing it for the first time. The packed theater of producers loved it. It was Guy's first foray into extensive special effects, and I thought he did a spectacular job.

Disney took notice and grabbed him for the live-action version of *Aladdin*. Somehow, he managed to inject his unique style into the world of singing genies and flying carpets.

"People don't really understand what goes into a sound mix. It's a massive part of filmmaking that takes forever and costs a fortune. You can only really enjoy the full audio experience at the cinema." Translation: Stop watching movies on your phone and go to the theater.

Guy is prolific, turning out several projects a year. Like all of us, he has had ups and downs. There is an expression: Don't hate the player, hate the game. Guy says, "Don't hate the game, love the game, because you're in it, mate. So own the game, accept the rules, and move on into the rules."

Richard Rush

Back in 1947, Richard was one of the first film students to emerge from the brand-new cinema department at UCLA. Fresh out of school, he wasted no time and started making TV programs for the U.S. military.

Richard is best known for directing *The Stunt Man*, starring Peter O'Toole—a film that earned him two Oscar nominations for Best Director and Best Screenplay. When Peter O'Toole read the screenplay, he called up Richard and said, "I'm a literate and intelligent man, as you know, and I won't beat around the bush, but if you don't give me this role, I'll kill you." Even François Truffaut couldn't resist weighing in; when asked who his favorite American director was, he replied, "I don't know his name, but I saw his film last night and it was called *The Stunt Man*." It has been called "every director's favorite film."

Off camera, Richard was an accomplished pilot. He'd often fly friends in his Cessna 421 to Mammoth for ski vacations. He and his wife, Claude, were known as great hosts and often entertained at their Bel Air home.

On a personal note, Richard and I shared the same wonderful sound design team, Dessie Markovsky and Emile Razpopov, a couple who became close friends over the years.

During his eclectic career, Richard directed Tab Hunter playing a serial killer in *The Fickle Finger of Fate*, and Merle Oberon playing a nymphomaniac in *Of Love and Desire*. He worked with Jack Nicholson early on in *Hells Angels on Wheels* and *Psych-Out*, and with the beach party girl Annette Funicello in *Thunder Alley*. Richard directed one of the earliest buddy-cop films, *Freebie and the Bean* (starring Alan Arkin and James Caan), and co-wrote the "buddy-pilot" comedy *Air America*, which became his biggest box-office hit.

In 1970, he directed *Getting Straight*, a film featuring a young Harrison Ford that even Ingmar Bergman proclaimed as "the best American film of the decade." Richard liked that.

His film *Color of Night* scooped up a Golden Raspberry Award for worst film in 1994. A dubious honor that Richard proudly displayed...in his bathroom. Years later, Maxim magazine hailed the same movie as having the best sex scene in film history. When I heard that, I had to see for myself. I guess times have changed, because it seemed tame by today's standards.

David O. Russell

When I was growing up, I got to know my father's boss, Helena Devereux. She ran a foundation for emotionally disturbed children in Devon, Pennsylvania, where my father was head of clinical psychology. We called her Miss Devereux, and under her leadership, her foundation expanded into many other schools. One of them, the Devereux Glenholme School in Connecticut, became the inspiration for David O. Russell's award-winning *Silver Linings Playbook*. With his son attending the school, David had a personal connection that allowed him to explore its dramatic and comedic possibilities with authenticity. The film earned eight Oscar nominations, including a win for Jennifer Lawrence. Since then, David has become an advocate for autism research.

David has made some compelling films, but my personal favorite is his Gulf War black comedy, *Three Kings*. It pulls off a tough balancing act—mixing drama, politics, and satire. Spike Jonze, a director himself, is hilarious playing one of the soldiers.

David often says his films have a distinct tone—rooted in friendship, love, and flawed outsiders—and that the humor comes from their sincerity. It's not that the characters are trying to be funny; it's that they're so genuine, their struggles and awkward moments naturally become comedic. His method for writing screenplays starts with him meticulously creating the story from each character's point of view, emphasizing their humanity and specific quirks.

David is relentless about leaving nothing to chance. That perfectionism has earned him a reputation for clashing with his actors. Despite on-set battles, he has led many of those actors to some of their best performances and, more than a few times, Oscar nominations.

Beyond his work in Hollywood, David is committed to supporting fresh talent. He backs the Ghetto Film School, an organization that teaches cinema to Latino and Black young filmmakers from Harlem and the South Bronx. It's the kind of initiative that helps voices that might otherwise go unheard find their place in the industry.

Mark Rydell

I originally got to know Mark and his wife, Esther, at soirees at the home of my friend Sally Kellerman. Later, I attended his in-depth seminars at the DGA, where he broke down the craft of directing.

Mark has had a long, multifaceted career as a director, musician, actor, and teacher. He originally studied piano, and found that experience relevant in acting and directing. It taught him the importance of dynamics and rhythm. "You can't pretend to be a musician. You learn and respect craft." That mindset carried into his film work. He studied at the Actors Studio alongside James Dean, Marlon Brando, and Paul Newman. I loved his performance as Jack Warner in the TV movie *James Dean*, which he also directed.

When Jane Fonda bought the play *On Golden Pond* as a way to reconnect with her father, he personally requested Mark to direct. Henry had admired Mark's earlier films, *The Reivers* and *The Cowboys*. On the first day of shooting, Katherine Hepburn decided to test Mark. She showed up in a stylish outfit not chosen for the scene. Mark calmly turned to the crew and said, "Everybody take ten. Miss Hepburn is about to go to her dressing room to put on the outfit we selected." She bristled, but relented and changed.

Mark once shared a powerful directing moment with me. In a key scene, Hepburn was supposed to bolster up Henry Fonda as his character realizes he is losing his faculties. During rehearsal, she was passionate and full of energy, but it wasn't working. She asked Mark what to do. He told her to whisper it in his ear, plant a seed of confidence. "You're my knight in shining armor." Fonda teared up. The scene became one of the best in the movie.

Mark had to fight hard for his brilliant casting of the then-unknown Bette Midler in *The Rose*, where she played a thinly disguised Janis Joplin. The studio wanted a star. Mark insisted. In retaliation, they cut his salary in half. A few weeks into the shooting, they reinstated it. Bette was riveting and inspiring in the film.

Over the years, Mark has shared some great insights about directing: "Psychoanalysis was very helpful in working with actors."... "It's not about dialogue, it's about behavior"... "What do the characters want from each other?"... Nothing is worth doing unless it's truthful."... "You want to reveal vulnerability and encourage intimacy"... "Sometimes you light the fire and stand back and let them burn."

Mark now lives at the Motion Picture Home in Woodland Hills, where I enjoy visiting him and hearing fascinating stories.

Joseph Sargent

I did this sketch during a DGA seminar that Joe gave for assistant directors wanting to move into directing.

Growing up in New Jersey, Joe made 8mm films at age 11 before joining the Actors Studio in New York. After acting on Broadway, he moved into directing classic series like *Bonanza* and *Star Trek*. He moved up to TV movies, earning nine Emmy nominations and winning four.

On the big screen, he delivered memorable films: Gregory Peck as the larger-than-life general in *MacArthur*, Burt Reynolds' high-octane ride in *White Lightning*, and his most popular work, *The Taking of Pelham One Two Three*. He described making *Pelham* as working in a coal mine. The cast and crew had to wear surgical masks because every time they moved a train, ancient dust and soot would be stirred up, creating an unbearable breathing situation.

I really enjoyed Joe's sci-fi thriller *Colossus: The Forbin Project*, written by my late friend James Bridges, who would go on to direct *The China Syndrome* and *Urban Cowboy*. *Colossus* was about two supercomputers, one American and one Russian, combining efforts to control humanity and prevent nuclear destruction. Their method is to demonstrate their power by blowing things up. It was AI ahead of its time, and well executed by Joe.

We all have our ups and downs. In 1987, Joe snagged a Razzie nomination for Worst Director in the 1987 Golden Raspberry Awards for *Jaws: The Revenge*. Tasked with "killing the shark in a different way that's never been done before," he opted to impale the shark with the boat's bowsprit. Joe later said, "How do grown men with good credentials get involved with something that idiotic? It still puzzles me. You think it's a great fresh approach, and you convince yourself it will work."

Joe had an unexpected connection to Stanley Kubrick. While directing a play featuring an actress Stanley was dating, Joe caught Kubrick's attention. Stanley began quietly attending rehearsals from the back of the theater and was struck by Joe's deep grasp of Stanislavski's Method. At the time, Kubrick was preparing to direct *One-Eyed Jacks* with Marlon Brando and brought Joe on as a consultant to immerse himself in the Method. After three months of collaboration, Kubrick stepped away from the project to take on *Spartacus*, and Brando ultimately directed the film himself.

After teaching at the American Film Institute, Joe wanted to be remembered not as someone who changed the world, but as "someone who made enough dents to change some minds."

Thomas Schlamme

Tommy Schlamme is a well-respected figure in the industry, served as DGA president for four years, and is married to the wonderful actress and filmmaker Christine Lahti. During the writer's strike, he stood in solidarity and made his stance clear: "I owe a great deal of my career to the incredible writers I've worked with. I'm here to tell you the DGA is completely behind you." He was absolutely right.

His path into the business was almost accidental. A high school jock, Tommy was on a football field in 110-degree heat when he heard the drama department had air conditioning. He joined the department, earned a theater scholarship, and changed his life.

He began his career in 1981, directing the first "I Want My MTV!" commercial. He made two comedies, his debut feature, *Miss Firecracker*, with Holly Hunter, and the quirky *So I Married an Axe Murderer*, starring Mike Myers. But he made his name in television, directing many TV series, including *Friends, Tracey Takes On..., ER, Mad About You, Chicago Hope,* and *House of Cards*. He also became an executive producer on *Snowfall*, a series initiated by my friend, the late John Singleton.

But his defining work came with *The West Wing*. Tommy collaborated with Aaron Sorkin and perfected the signature "walk and talk" technique—many pages of dialogue are captured in one moving shot, with characters weaving in and out of frame. As he explained to The Hollywood Reporter, "You almost never see how anyone travels from point A to point C (in most TV shows). I wanted the audience to witness every journey these people took. It all had a purpose, even seeing them order lunch. It just seemed to be the proper visual rhythm with which to marry Aaron's words. I got lucky that it worked." His *luck* really defined that show and influenced so many others.

After four seasons, tensions with the network surfaced, and Sorkin and Tommy left the show. Comedian Larry David, in his typical brutally honest fashion, told Sorkin never to watch the show again. Why? Because either they killed his baby, or they made it better. His main wish for the future of TV directors is fewer notes from the networks and studios. As he puts it, "They often can't remember what their first idea was."

His advice to newcomers: "Throw yourself into whatever your job is. Be the best P.A. Then you'll move up. It's alchemy, not chemistry."

Julian Schnabel

Besides being a director, Julian is a celebrated artist. He often does large-scale paintings using diverse materials and combining figurative and abstract elements. His work is on display at many of the world's top museums. "I feel more alive when I'm creating art."

His fascination with fellow visual artists led to two landmark films. First came *Basquiat*, in which he cast David Bowie as Andy Warhol and gave Jeffrey Wright the title role, launching his career. Julian had a personal connection to the material: "I knew Basquiat. I was in that basement where he worked."

The second film exploring other artists was *At Eternity's Gate*, a biopic of Vincent Van Gogh. Initially reluctant, he identified with Van Gogh's own credo, "I am my paintings." Julian believed the public's perception of Van Gogh needed a more accurate and genuine portrayal. His screenplay has several unforgettable lines: "A grain of madness is the best of art," and "Maybe God made me a painter for people who aren't born yet." To bring Van Gogh to life, Julian even taught Willem Dafoe the fundamentals of painting so the actor would move and see like the master himself.

In his Oscar-nominated film *The Diving Bell and the Butterfly*, Julian plunges us into the locked-in world of a stroke patient. A subtle yet powerful visual effect: showing the character's eyelids opening and closing with each blink, makes the isolation visceral. Watching this movie, I realized how devastating this affliction must be. The idea that communication is cut off, save for those blinks, is terrifying. It really hit home for me, as I remember spending time with dear John Schlesinger, who sadly suffered the same way. Julian made the situation vividly come to life.

Earlier in his career, Julian directed Javier Bardem in *Before Night Falls*, the story of a persecuted gay Cuban writer who eventually ends his life in New York. A performance that earned Bardem his first Oscar nomination.

Julian's latest film, *In the Hand of Dante*, continues his fascination with artists wrestling with their inner worlds. This time, bridging Dante Alighieri's medieval journey with a modern story. The film features great performances from Oscar Isaac and Al Pacino.

"Whether it's a screen in a movie or a rectangle, that's the perimeter of a painting, it's an arena where this battle takes place between everything you know and don't know, and forms who you are."

Artur Allan Seidelman

Arthur directed Arnold Schwarzenegger's first film, *Hercules Goes Bananas*, and staged a chariot race around Times Square. It was his first film. We won't hold it against him. He claims he was 12 at the time and got paid $1,000 per week plus cheese sandwiches.

Since then, he's had a prolific and varied career, directing features, operas, Broadway shows, TV movies, and episodes of classic series like *Fame*, *The Paper Chase*, *Knots Landing*, *Hill Street Blues*, *Magnum, P.I.*, *Murder, She Wrote*, *Trapper John, M.D.*, and *L.A. Law*.

When I interviewed him for the DGA Visual History Program, he shared a painful and funny anecdote. He was directing a TV show, and his mentor, Sanford Meisner, visited the set. As luck would have it, the producers had saddled Arthur with a very bad actor who was blowing take after take. Meisner called Arthur and quietly asked, "And what do you do here?" Arthur said it was somewhat in jest, but he wanted to sink into the floor.

Arthur's never been one to shy away from speaking his mind, especially with studio executives. Once, a Disney executive dismissed his input by saying, "We own the negative. We don't need to hear your thoughts anymore." Arthur shot back, "You may own the negative, but you didn't create it. And if you're too stupid not to listen to my suggestions, then it's your loss, not mine. Sequences I shoot work no matter how you butcher them. So do you want to hear my suggestion or not, you arrogant lady?" Then he quoted Billy Wilder: "Theirs is the kingdom and the power, but ours is the glory."

While directing Elizabeth Taylor in *Poker Alice*, Arthur found himself out of time and struggling to stage a scene with her and Tom Skerritt. He wanted to do it in a "oner" with no coverage, but couldn't figure out how. Taylor saw what he was attempting and made it happen. Arthur said she taught him a valuable lesson that day: sometimes, the best thing a director can do is simply get out of the way.

Arthur stays up on the latest tech and is a member of our Digital Day committee at the DGA.

You can find a link to my interview with Arthur at www.randalkleiser.com

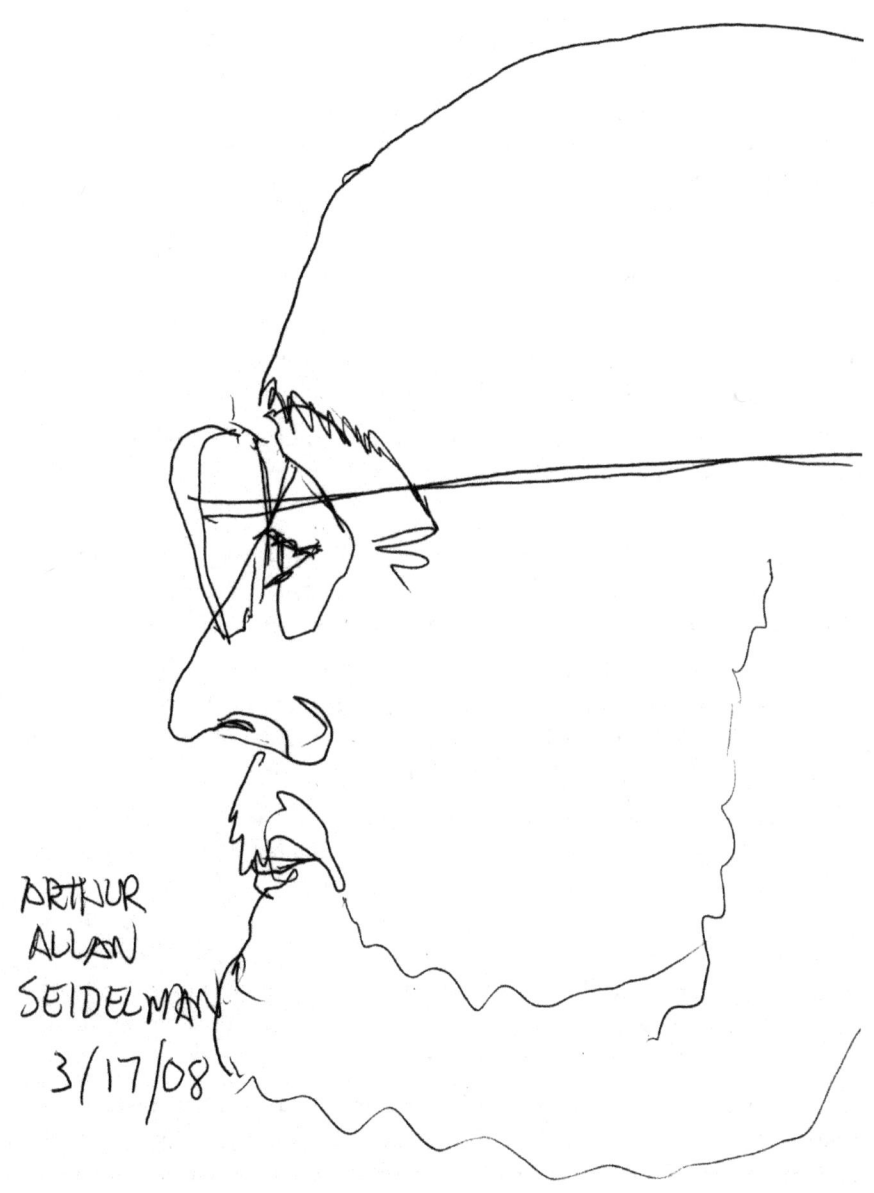

Andy Serkis

I was astounded when I saw Andy Serkis' performance as Gollum in *The Lord of the Rings*. The first truly believable CGI character in cinema history. Initially, Peter Jackson planned to cast Gollum with a voice actor, relying entirely on CGI. But after witnessing Andy's uncanny physicality, his eerie, contorted movements, and vocal nuances, Jackson changed course on the spot and decided to experiment with the then-nascent technology of motion capture. The rest is history.

From there, he went on to create many more groundbreaking characters, the title role in *King Kong*, the lead ape Caesar in the new *Planet of the Apes* series, and the sinister Snoke in the *Star Wars* saga.

To play King Kong, he wore a gorilla muscle suit and perched atop cranes, cherry pickers, and adjustable ladders to hit the right eyeline opposite Naomi Watts.

In a smart move, he parlayed his unique experiences into launching a motion capture studio, The Imaginarium. Using this innovative facility, he directed and starred in *Mowgli: Legend of the Jungle* and *Animal Farm*.

I was quite impressed with his handling of the mega-budget Marvel/Sony sequel, *Venom: Let There Be Carnage*. The action sequences and visual effects are suitably over-the-top, and Andy coaxed wonderfully twisted performances from Tom Hardy and Woody Harrelson.

Years ago, I remember seeing him projected live from London at the Academy Theater for a seminar on performance capture many years ago. It was one of the first live videoconferences I'd seen. Andy explained the burgeoning technology in understandable language, detailing how directors first work with actors on the performance and later collaborate with the animators on creating the visuals that bring the performance to life. Andy was able to clearly explain how you can add layer upon layer of detail, sometimes over months, to get the perfect result.

Whether in front of or behind the camera, Andy keeps surprising me—I enjoyed his take on Alfred the Butler in *The Batman*. His work continues to push the envelope, making him one of the most dynamic talents in the industry.

Brad Silberling

I often chatted with Brad before and after meetings at the DGA and found him to be personable and low-key.

On the day *Jaws* was released, Brad showed up at the 11 AM screening and was blown away. He rushed home, grabbed his dad's Super 8 camera, and began making films. He was 12.

His career took off when his UCLA thesis film made its way to Universal, which offered him a term deal. Brad started directing TV, and an episode of *Brooklyn Bridge* caught Steven Spielberg's attention. Steven offered him the directing job on *Casper*. Brad was nervous because if it tanked, he would never get a second picture. But Steven encouraged him to take the leap and even showed up on the first day of shooting. *Casper* was a hit, and it opened the door to more features.

He got a supportive note from Dustin Hoffman, "I can tell you like actors." Brad was impressed enough to offer Dustin a role in his most personal film. While at film school, Brad had been dating actress Rebecca Schaeffer when she was murdered by an obsessed fan. Out of that grief came *Moonlight Mile*, an emotional drama he wrote and directed. He cast my former neighbor, Jake Gyllenhaal, to play his younger self, alongside Dustin Hoffman and Susan Sarandon as the girl's parents.

After watching Wim Wenders' *Wings of Desire*, Brad was so affected, he couldn't get out of his seat. He thought it was a masterpiece. When approached to direct the remake, he hesitated until he learned that Wenders fully supported it. Brad set the story in Los Angeles and retitled it *City of Angels*.

Brad received great reviews for the offbeat fantasy film, *Lemony Snicket's A Series of Unfortunate Events*. To establish a working rapport with Jim Carrey, Brad used a technique he'd heard John Schlesinger employed on *Midnight Cowboy:* a series of in-character interviews that allowed the actor to explore the role through conversation. During production, Brad became overwhelmed with stress and left the Paramount set to get some air. As he walked around the lot, he heard walkie-talkies blaring, "Don't let him get to Melrose."

"No matter what the budget is, twenty thousand or two hundred million, showing it to an audience is the great equalizer. Do they like it or not?"

Elliot Silverstein

When I joined the Directors Guild in 1973, I was fortunate to meet and spend time with Elliot Silverstein. He was a trailblazer who fought to give directors the right to have a "Director's Cut," both in film and television.

The turning point came when Elliot directed an episode of *The Twilight Zone*, and the editor refused to cut a scene the way Elliot had envisioned, bluntly stating, "I don't want to cut it that way." Frustrated, Elliot talked to other directors and realized they were also facing similar resistance from studios and editors. Determined to bring about change, he became a member of the Guild's newly formed Creative Rights Committee, leading the fight to establish essential protections for directors. He was joined by heavyweights like Frank Capra, Robert Altman, and Sidney Pollack, and together, they reshaped industry standards. We all owe a great debt to these pioneers who stood up for creative control and artistic integrity.

Elliot's own credits are just as impressive. He's best known for *Cat Ballou*, the uproarious comedy-western that gave Jane Fonda the title role and showcased Lee Marvin's unforgettable dual performance as both a fearsome hired gun and his twin brother—a perpetually drunk cowboy whose antics stole the show. Under Elliot's direction, Marvin nailed every beat, from sharp physical comedy to moments of genuine drama. In his Best Actor acceptance speech, Marvin famously *donated* half of his Oscar to his scene-stealing horse.

On a totally different note, and showing his versatility, I remember Elliot's serious western, *A Man Called Horse*. He staged one of the most harrowing sequences I've ever seen: Richard Harris is strung up by his chest with two hooks during a Sioux initiation rite. Hard to watch. To this day, I still can't figure out how he pulled off this visceral scene.

In an interview, Elliot recalled a heartbreaking moment during one of his *Twilight Zone* episodes. An actor playing an old man with a dying wife was, in real life, going through the same tragedy. In the middle of a three-day schedule, "his wife did in fact die." The actor, a true professional, held off mourning until the episode wrapped.

Beyond filmmaking, his advocacy didn't stop at the Guild. He founded the Artist Rights Foundation, which later became the Film Foundation, continuing his lifelong fight for directors' rights.

In recognition of his contributions, the DGA honored him with the Robert B. Aldrich Achievement Award in 1985 and an Honorary Lifetime Member Award in 1990. I'll always remember how he warmly greeted and supported me when I first joined the Guild.

Aaron Sorkin

I first became aware of Aaron Sorkin when I attended his Broadway play *A Few Good Men*—a completely captivating story that impressed as much as his later movie adaptation.

I sketched Aaron during the promotional tour for his directorial debut, *Molly's Game*. Jessica Chastain gave a terrific performance as the lead, a real-life poker impresario who ran an underground gambling club that was eventually busted by the FBI.

Aaron started out as a theater major who began working as a bartender at the Palace Theatre on Broadway to make ends meet. In his spare time, he started writing *A Few Good Men* on cocktail napkins during the first act of *La Cage aux Folles*. He assumed he would just get some actor friends to read it in his apartment. Through a lucky set of circumstances, David Brown agreed to the Broadway run, even though he'd been strictly a movie producer until then.

Aaron's series *The West Wing* was born during a lunch with producer John Wells. Aaron, caught off guard, pitched a White House series on the spot using leftover material from his previous screenplay, *The American President*. He worked with director Tommy Schlamme, and they developed their signature style, long uninterrupted takes of actors doing dialogue as they walk.

For *Steve Jobs*, rather than doing a biopic, Aaron created three pivotal 40-minute scenes, each centered on a product launch, to chart Jobs' evolution over time.

Aaron is most comfortable, as a writer and now as a director, in scenes set inside four walls: people talking in rooms. His directorial style is saying yes to people when they come up with a good idea. He has received multiple Academy Award nominations and won for *The Social Network*.

I was pleasantly surprised by his film, *Being the Ricardos*, where he uncovered a little-known scandal: Lucille Ball was wrongly accused of being a communist. This political and historical twist added layers of depth to the movie. My favorite sequence was when Nicole Kidman, as Lucy, analyzes how to pull off a gag and then performs it in its final form. It really showed how much of a comic genius Lucy was.

"Bad times generally produce good art. So we can look forward to that, I have a hunch."

Douglas Day Stewart

My friendship with Doug goes way, way back. I first met him when we were both assigned to the TV movie *The Boy in the Plastic Bubble*. The original script focused on the parents of a Texas boy born with no immune system, but Doug saw the real story in the child's perspective and shifted the entire narrative around him. Thanks to producer Joel Thurm's persistence, we landed John Travolta, the up-and-coming TV star from *Welcome Back, Kotter*, for his first leading role. The movie went on to win Emmys and earned a devoted cult following. I still remember John accepting Diana Hyland's posthumous Emmy on her behalf. She had been his partner before losing her battle with breast cancer.

Years later, when my mentor Frank Price greenlit *The Blue Lagoon* at Columbia, I knew exactly whom to call. Doug transformed Henry de Vere Stacpoole's Victorian novel into a coming-of-age tale and made it work for the 1980s audience. Doug was able to delve into areas the novelist dared not go in his era. How would isolated children deal with puberty with no understanding of what was happening to their bodies? This perspective resonated with young filmgoers. Even now, many people come up to me and say it was the movie that previewed and explained their own adolescent development.

Doug came to the Fijian islands, where he polished the script as we discovered new elements in the landscape, often inspired by the genius eye of our cinematographer, Néstor Almendros.

Doug then directed *Thief of Hearts*, a tense thriller about a man who steals a woman's diary and then stalks her, followed by the drama *Listen to Me*, about college debaters. But his signature achievement remains the semi-autobiographical original screenplay for *An Officer and a Gentleman*, which earned him an Oscar nomination. He later adapted it into a stage musical—a production I saw in Las Vegas. Louis Gossett, Jr., who won the Oscar for playing Sergeant Foley in the film version, was in the audience to support Doug. During the climactic scene, when Officer Zack Mayo picks up Paula and carries her out of the factory to the famous ballad, "Up Where We Belong," the entire audience rose to their feet.

In 2024, Doug revisited that world with his novelization sequel, *An Officer's Daughter*. I was proud to moderate the Q and A for him at a book signing in Brentwood.

Almost five decades into our friendship, he's still the first person I call for script advice.

Jacques Tati

During my film studies at USC, I discovered the delightful films of Jacques Tati. Much like Charlie Chaplin gave life to his Tramp character, Jacques Tati created the iconic Monsieur Hulot—an endearingly clumsy everyman. In *Mon Oncle*, his goofy bumbling collides with the sleek gadgetry of an ultra-modern '50s home. In *Monsieur Hulot's Holiday*, he explores eccentric characters interacting at a French beach resort. Monsieur Hulot's films don't rely much on plot; they are a series of vignettes that exude playfulness and joy.

In one sequence of his film *Traffic*, Jacques artfully combined music with abstract imagery in ways that no doubt inspired my friend George Lucas' early student film, *Herbie*.

One of the things I love most about Jacques' cinematic style is his use of wide, static shots to play with sound effects presented like a naked foley track. His oddball characters could meander through meticulously designed sets, punctuating each move with precisely timed sound effects, creating a unique comedic effect. His cinematic visual style created comedy beats that remind one of the early works of Buster Keaton, but Jacques' focus on the absurdities of contemporary life and offbeat characters is entirely his own. You can see an overview on YouTube at "The Most Beautiful Shots of Jacques Tati's Movies."

Tati's observations about modern life and offbeat characters set him apart from any other filmmaker. He built a massive full-scale replica of a glass and steel metropolis for his epic, *Playtime*. As the film went over budget, he refused to compromise his vision. He ended up going bankrupt.

As a film student, I was absolutely thrilled to attend a screening of *Playtime* at Grauman's Chinese Theater and actually get within a few feet of him as he was mobbed leaving the theater.

Decades after his death, in 2010, director Sylvain Chomet brought Jacques' spirit back with the animated film *The Illusionist*, based on a screenplay by Jacques Tati. The Monsieur Hulot persona was reborn as the central animated character, ensuring that his unique charm continues to inspire new generations.

Norman Taurog

Norman cast me in a bit with Elvis Presley.

At the tail end of his long directing career, Norman began teaching at USC, where I was a film student moonlighting as a movie extra. One of his last movies was *Double Trouble*, and he added me to a disco sequence as a dance extra. During the musical number "Baby, If You'll Give Me All Your Love," he orchestrated a moment where Elvis walks up to my partner and me, pulls her up onstage for a short dance, and then returns her to me. (You can see the scene below.)

Norman's directing class quickly became one of my favorites. He loved sharing stories about techniques he had used over the years, often funny, sometimes jaw-dropping. One that left a lasting impression was from *Skippy*. He told us how, to make his 8-year-old nephew, Jackie Coogan, cry on cue, he asked the security guard to take Jackie's dog behind a truck and shoot off a blank pistol. The trick worked: Jackie earned the youngest-ever Oscar nomination for a lead role, and Norman became the youngest winner for Best Director. Today, such a tactic would be unimaginable. It left a lasting impression on Jackie, who later recounted it in his memoir, *Please Don't Shoot My Dog*. Another time, during the filming of *We're Not Dressing*, Norman needed Bing Crosby to swim in a studio tank. Crosby dipped his hand into the cold water, declared he wouldn't do the scene until it was heated, and then retreated to his dressing room. Norman asked the prop man to throw dry ice into the water to create a layer of smoke, then called Crosby out of his trailer and had him jump in the frigid tank. He faced Crosby's fury, but he got the shot.

Norman's long career began in the silent era with dozens of shorts, many of them featuring extremely dangerous stunts. He briefly worked on *The Wizard of Oz* before being replaced by George Cukor and then Victor Fleming. He specialized in comedy, directing six films with Jerry Lewis and Dean Martin, and nine movies with Elvis Presley.

Thanks to my Elvis adventure, Norman gets my vote as the coolest professor at USC.

You can view the scene from *Double Trouble* at youtu.be/3ZYpodqUQ6g

Brian Trenchard-Smith

Even though I've known Brian for years through DGA events, I never realized he had been crowned the "Ozploitation King."

He started his show business career making TV promos and trailers. His love for old movie magazines made him publish his own in Australia. The first issue featured a bloody face on the cover. His friends said no one would buy a magazine with such an image. Brian knew better.

Violence became a trademark of his work, catching the attention of Quentin Tarantino, who considers Brian one of his favorite directors. Quentin even interviewed him for the documentary *Not Quite Hollywood: The Wild, Untold Story of Ozploitation!*

In his frontier filmmaking days in Australia, Brian often performed his own stunts. In fact, he set himself on fire seven times, even once to reassure an actor that it was completely safe. Unfortunately, that actor ended up with a severe burn on his hand.

I loved Brian's book, *Adventures in the B Movie Trade*. He mentions the first time he met Quentin: "I gave my name and he said: 'You made *Turkey Shoot!*' He went on: 'I loved that scene where the Guard from Hell beats that girl to death on the parade ground while she tries to recite the dissident's mea culpa.' Which Quentin then recited verbatim!"

There was a notorious scene of an exploding head in *Turkey Shoot* that the MPAA demanded be cut. Brian edited it out of one print but left it intact in the versions that went out to the theaters. He got caught and had to remove it from all the prints. To get back at the censors, Brian included the shot in a later film, *Dead End Drive-In*, where it appears on the drive-in screen.

Though known for raunchy, violent exploitation films, Brian has a broader range. *BMX Bandits* featured a then-unknown fifteen-year-old Nicole Kidman. On set, they jokingly called her "the beanpole" and "the mop." The producers didn't want to cast her because she was taller than the two male leads, but Brian saw her potential. Brian suggested Nicole for the Aussie series *Five Mile Creek*, where he ended up directing her second episode. Back then, he predicted she would become Australia's Katharine Hepburn. Soon after, Nicole broke out in Phillip Noyce's *Dead Calm*, and her career took off.

Brian also directed *The Quest*, a children's adventure film starring *E.T.*'s Henry Thomas. He still has personal projects he wants to make, but as far as accepting directing assignments: "I've never met a greenlight I didn't like."

Gus Van Sant

Gus has been described as a "hipster Stanley Kubrick." I met him at a dinner party hosted by photographer Greg Gorman, which turned out to be a gathering of the so-called Velvet Mafia: John Schlesinger, David Hockney, Ian McKellen, Bryan Singer, and John Waters. With so many Type-A personalities, Gus and I remained fairly quiet.

Early in his career, Gus was influenced by the indie style of filmmakers like John Sayles and John Waters. He made his mark directing groundbreaking indie films such as *Mala Noche*, a love story between a Mexican immigrant and a gay clerk; *Drugstore Cowboy*, about young junkies robbing drugstores, which really put him on the map; and later the very challenging *Elephant*, which bravely explored the Columbine shootings.

Inspired by Stanley Kubrick's unconventional screenplays, Gus wrote *My Own Private Idaho* in a freeform style—filled with poems, drawings, and mixed fonts—breaking Hollywood's rigid formatting rules and initially baffling studios. Gus sent the script to River Phoenix and Keanu Reeves, not expecting them to say yes. To his surprise, they both agreed. My good friend Tom Troupe played the father of Keanu's character, a man who disapproved of his son's lifestyle.

When River read the script, the campfire scene stood out to him. He asked Gus to shoot it from four angles in a single take. Gus agreed—and the result is one of the most powerful scenes in the film. Gus' fascinating novel, Pink, is a thinly veiled exploration of his grief over River Phoenix's death.

Good Will Hunting was Gus' most commercial picture. Regarding directing Matt Damon, he said, "Matt can do anything you ask, and can pick up on your emotions and give you what you want."

After a screening of his thriller *Dead Man's Wire*, Gus shared with me that the final version was very close to the first rough cut. The film was shot in 19 days with 5 cameras, and the cut played well, with laughs he had not anticipated. He decided not to go back into all the takes to polish what was already working.

My favorite of his films is *Milk*, with its tremendous suspense and important message. Gus drew what I believe to be the best performance of Sean Penn's career, resulting in the Best Actor Oscar. My friend Dustin Lance Black won the Oscar for Best Screenplay and gave an extremely moving acceptance speech.

Francis Veber

I sketched this at the City of Lights, City of Angels Festival at the DGA in 2021. Francis Veber interviewed Jacqueline Bisset after a screening of *Le Magnifique*, a spy spoof she co-starred with Jean-Paul Belmondo. I was in awe watching the interview. For me, Jacqueline will always be a star from Francois Truffaut's *Day for Night*, a movie about making movies, and one of my favorites from my film school days.

Francis is a French film director, screenwriter, producer, and playwright who has created the source material for more American remakes than anyone else. The French films he was involved with were picked up by Hollywood and rebooted with American casts. It's an impressive list: *The Man with One Red Shoe, Buddy Buddy, The Birdcage, The Toy, Fathers' Day, Pure Luck, Three Fugitives, Dinner for Schmucks,* and *The Valet* all began as Francis originals. His scripts often echo Neil Simon comedies, featuring two totally opposite characters forced by circumstance to engage with one another. Several of his projects originally began as stage plays, a format that allowed him to fine-tune dialogue based on immediate audience reactions.

Francis' movies are typically under 90 minutes, and his writing and directing have been described as "marvels of economy." When asked about the most important lesson he had learned about writing, he replied, "You need to read your script to your close friends. See if they are bored. If they are honest, they will tell you it's bad."

One of his idols, Billy Wilder, adapted Francis' screenplay *L'emmerdeur* into *Buddy Buddy*. Although Francis was thrilled that the writers behind classics like *Sunset Boulevard* and *Some Like It Hot* were working on one of his projects, he was disappointed with the final draft, which he thought was "quite bad." Francis agonized over how to tell his hero that the script didn't work. At last, he summoned the courage to call, but as he started to make a suggestion, Wilder cut him off and refused to make any changes. Francis simply wished him luck. Unfortunately, the film became both a critical and commercial flop.

Continuing the family legacy, his son Jean Veber directs films and hosts a podcast on cinema, carrying on his father's passion for storytelling.

David S. Ward

David Ward is another USC success story, though to be perfectly fair, he also studied at UCLA. In 1973, he won the Best Original Screenplay Oscar for *The Sting*. That triumph opened the door to directing. His first feature was an adaptation of John Steinbeck's intertwined tales, *Cannery Row* and *Sweet Thursday*. Having spent two summers painting houses in the actual Cannery Row while he was a film student, David knew the setting intimately and treated the novels' episodic structure as a single narrative.

The studio insisted on casting a marquee name and signed Raquel Welch. She was not David's first choice, and he told her she had to come across like a regular person, without glamor. On the first day, Raquel spent 3 hours in makeup and criticized his first shot. David begged the studio to fire her. They agreed, recast with Debra Winger, and reshot the first three days. Nick Nolte, who starred as Doc, got great reviews for his performance.

I remember in 1981 stopping by the MGM lot in Culver City and noticing that David's production designer Richard MacDonald was ingeniously using the archways between the soundstages as a stand-in for Monterey's historic canneries.

Robert Redford, who starred in *The Sting*, later acquired the rights to John Nichols' novel *The Milagro Beanfield War* and asked David to adapt it. The film, centered on a battle about water rights, received interesting reviews for its humanistic themes and touch of magical realism. Its success enabled David to secure support for a comedy he'd been pitching for years, *Major League*. It explored the theme of underdogs coming out on top, which he revisited in *King Ralph*, where John Goodman improbably becomes King of England, and *Major League II*.

David earned another Oscar nomination, this time for co-writing the romantic hit, *Sleepless in Seattle*. The script was based on a story by Jeff Arch and directed by the late Nora Ephron.

The industry is all about relationships, and they often come full circle. Tony Bill, who produced *The Sting*, reconnected with David in 2005 and got him involved in writing *Flyboys*, a fighter pilot drama set in World War I.

In 2010, I was invited to be the Filmmaker-In-Residence at Dodge College at Chapman University in Orange County. I ran into David, who was then teaching, directing, and leading the screenwriting program. He is popular among the students, many of whom thank him in their student film credit rolls for his mentorship.

Orson Welles

In the late sixties at USC Cinema, George Lucas and I, like all film students, studied *Citizen Kane*, often hailed as the greatest movie ever made. We screened Welles' other classics, including *The Magnificent Ambersons, The Lady from Shanghai*, and *Touch of Evil*. We listened to the famously hilarious recording of Orson being "directed" for a radio commercial, and we were well aware of his notorious radio stunt with *War of the Worlds*. To us, he was a hero.

A little over a decade later, Orson Welles came to a USC event. By then, George and I had become professionals, and the organizers arranged for us to meet him. At the private cocktail reception, three chairs were set up, and we were seated facing each other. The music was loud, and the other guests swarmed in to surround our chairs, leaning in to overhear what was said. The conversation was stilted and awkward, to say the least, and lasted less than ten minutes. It would have been terrific to have a quiet room and no crowd to really get to talk with this legend. That would never happen.

When you could hear him, he had great insights: "The job of a director is to discover in the actor something more than he knew he had." Orson also disdained imitation: "The most detestable habit in all of modern cinema is the homage. I don't want to see another goddamn homage in anybody's movie."

Years after his death, our classmate Walter Murch restored the butchered cut of *Touch of Evil* using Welles' own notes. The film had been mangled by the studio. Sadly, this was not the first time something like this had happened to Orson. *The Magnificent Ambersons* is another disturbing example of studio interference.

At a birthday party for Louis B. Mayer at the Hillcrest Country Club, Orson smuggled a rabbit under his coat. He was standing by to do a magic trick. So many stars entertained that night, Judy Garland, Danny Kaye, and Al Jolson. The party went on until dawn. The rabbit peed all over Orson, and he never did the trick.

On a personal note, when I directed Jeanette Nolan in my Master's Thesis film *Peege*, there was no IMDb to tell me that she played opposite Orson in *Macbeth*. Had I known, I would have been very intimidated.

Orson Welles was one of the greatest filmmakers of all time. When he passed, it was, paraphrasing Don McLean, "the day the movies died."

Joe Wright

I did this sketch when Joe was on the Academy Awards circuit promoting his film *Darkest Hour*. The screening was held at the Soho House, followed by an elegant cocktail party. The film received six Oscar nominations, including Best Picture, and Gary Oldman won Best Actor for his amazing portrayal of Sir Winston Churchill. The Oscar-winning make-up was so well done that Oldman was completely unrecognizable. When I met him at the reception afterward, he came across as remarkably down to earth.

Joe began his directing career with music videos before making his first feature, *Pride & Prejudice*, starring Keira Knightley. That film earned four Oscar nominations. He reunited with Knightley on *Atonement*, which garnered seven Oscar nominations, and in Joe's own words, is the film people should watch first from his body of work.

A passionate painter, Joe often composes his shots inspired by classical art. He also cites fellow Brit and film giant David Lean as a major influence on his work. You can see his good eye in the dynamics and stylish visuals of his action thriller, *Hanna*.

After tackling the dramas *The Soloist* and *Anna Karenina*, Joe ventured into a new genre with the large-scale musical fantasy *Pan*, a prequel to the *Peter Pan* story. Despite its impressive visual effects and production design, the film broke Joe's run of well-reviewed movies.

Joe returned in full force to the musical genre with his brilliant adaptation of *Cyrano* and the imaginative casting of Peter Dinklage. It's my favorite of his films. Lavish production values, excellent music, and perfectly staged scenes combine to create a moving story. On a Collider podcast, Joe confided that his connection to the title character was deeply personal. As a teenager, he felt odd and unlovable, and even today, he has trouble feeling worthy of love.

"Filmmaking is about reacting and adapting." During the *Cyrano* shoot, he was high up on a volcanic mountain when an unexpected snowstorm covered the set. He had to quickly restage the scenes, and on the last day of shooting, the volcano erupted, and the cast and crew had to run away.

Joe was happy to return to television with the series *The Agency*, drawn by the excellent writing. Although the show is set in the present, its characters and plot feel timeless.

"Out of specificity comes universality."

Jerry Zucker

In the '70s, I used to watch Jerry, his brother David, and their partner Jim Abrahams doing live improv skits—intercut with video clips—at the Kentucky Fried Theater on Pico Boulevard, just next to 20th Century Fox Studios. They'd actually started the ZAZ (Zucker, Abrahams, Zucker) shtick when they were students at the University of Wisconsin, making short films. By 1977, the trio had adapted their sketches into their first film, *Kentucky Fried Movie*. "We became directors out of self-defense. We didn't want anyone messing up our comedy."

The success of their debut led to the comedy classic *Airplane!*, for which my good friend Joel Thurm served as casting director. The Zucker brothers and Jim Abrahams cast traditionally straight-laced actors like Leslie Nielsen, Lloyd Bridges, and Peter Graves to play comedy for the first time.

Their follow-up, *Top Secret!*, starred Val Kilmer and included a hilarious spoof of my film *The Blue Lagoon*. In a surreal scene, lookalikes of Chris Atkins and Brooke Shields live on a bizarre island where they fish for bananas, go to the supermarket, and build a grass hut with an electric garage door. The parody ends with a mock-lovemaking scene that turns into a tangle of hands and feet.

I also loved the snarky charm of *Ruthless People,* in which Bette Midler's character learns her kidnapping ransom has been lowered and complains, "Do I understand this correctly? I'm being 'marked down'? What is this? The Bargain Basement?" This was a favorite movie of mine, and years later, I met the production designer and ended up buying the RV used in this movie for the hilarious scenes between Bill Pullman and Anita Morris.

Jerry was one of the first people to see my virtual reality project *Defrost,* and truly appreciated the new format and its potential: "It made me imagine new ways to tell short stories in a brand new form."

Beyond filmmaking, Jerry and his wife helped found the Science & Technology Exchange, a group that connects the entertainment industry with real-world experts to improve accuracy and to educate audiences. Jerry is also active in the Political Action Committee at the Directors Guild, where he regularly welcomes U.S. senators and members of Congress to our hosted lunches, never missing the chance to inject his trademark humor into the proceedings.

His best piece of advice for up-and-coming filmmakers: "Be as lucky as you possibly can."

Directory

Foreword 5
JJ Abrams 8
Ben Affleck 10
Fede Álvarez 12
Ken Annakin 14
Darren Aronofsky 16
Jacques Audiard 18
John Badham 20
Paul Bartel 22
Michael Bay 24
Warren Beatty 26
Robert Benton 28
Kathryn Bigelow 30
Peter Bogdanovich 32
Mel Brooks 34
James Burrows 36
Gil Cates 38
Jeremiah Chechik 40
Michael Cimino 42
Roman Coppola 44
Brady Corbet 46
Costa-Gavras 48
Kevin Costner 50
George Cukor 52
Joe Dante 54
Jonathan Dayton & Valerie Faris 56
Cecil B. DeMille 58
Brian De Palma 60
Howard Deutch 62

Stanley Donen	64
Richard Donner	66
Roland Emmerich	68
Federico Fellini	70
Gary Fleder	72
John Frankenheimer	74
Howard Franklin	76
Richard Franklin	78
Stephen Gaghan	80
Greta Gerwig	82
Mel Gibson	84
Terry Gilliam	86
Michael Goi	88
Michael Gracey	90
Christopher Guest	92
Randa Haines	94
Curtis Harrington	96
Anthony Harvey	98
Todd Haynes	100
Matthew Heineman	102
Werner Herzog	104
Tom Hooper	106
Reginald Hudlin	108
John Huston	110
Peter Hyams	112
Mick Jackson	114
Peter Jackson	116
Jim Jarmusch	118
Rian Johnson	120
Spike Jonze	122
Jonathan Kaplan	124
Joanna Kerns	126

Regina King	128
Stanley Kramer	130
John Landis	132
Yorgos Lanthimos	134
Pablo Larraín	136
David Lean	138
Mimi Leder	140
Claude Lelouch	142
Rob Lieberman	144
Richard Linklater	146
Joshua Logan	148
Sidney Lumet	150
David Lynch	152
Jonathan Lynn	154
James Mangold	156
Delbert Mann	158
Tom McCarthy	160
Charles McDougall	162
Robert Ellis Miller	164
George Miller	166
Vincente Minnelli	168
Lin-Manuel Miranda	170
Paul Morrissey	172
Jonathan Mostow	174
Phillip Noyce	176
Kenny Ortega	178
Daniel Petrie	180
Donald Petrie	182
William Phelps	184
Jeremy Podeswa	186
Roman Polanski	188
Otto Preminger	190

Irving Rapper 192
Peyton Reed 194
Carl Reiner 196
Gene Reynolds 198
John Rich 200
Guy Ritchie 202
Richard Rush 204
David O. Russell 206
Mark Rydell 208
Joseph Sargent 210
Thomas Schlamme 212
Julian Schnabel 214
Artur Allan Seidelman 216
Andy Serkis 218
Brad Silberling 220
Elliot Silverstein 222
Aaron Sorkin 224
Douglas Day Stewart 226
Jacques Tati 228
Norman Taurog 230
Brian Trenchard-Smith 232
Gus Van Sant 234
Francis Veber 236
David S. Ward 238
Orson Welles 240
Joe Wright 242
Jerry Zucker 244

www.ingramcontent.com/pod-product-compliance
Lightning Source LLC
LaVergne TN
LVHW010159070526
838199LV00062B/4425